THE

POWER

OF

understanding

YOURSELF

THE

POWER

OF

understanding

YOURSELF

THE KEY TO **SELF-DISCOVERY, PERSONAL DEVELOPMENT,** AND **BEING THE BEST YOU**

DAVE MITCHELL

WILEY

For general information on our other products and services or for technical support, please contact our Customer Care Department within the United States at (800) 762-2974, outside the United States at (317) 572-3993 or fax (317) 572-4002.

Wiley publishes in a variety of print and electronic formats and by print-on-demand. Some material included with standard print versions of this book may not be included in e-books or in print-on-demand. If this book refers to media such as a CD or DVD that is not included in the version you purchased, you may download this material at http://booksupport.wiley.com. For more information about Wiley products, visit www.wiley.com.

Library of Congress Cataloging-in-Publication Data:

Names: Mitchell, Dave, 1961- author.

Title: The power of understanding yourself : the key to self-discovery,

    personal development, and being the best you / Dave Mitchell.

Description: Hoboken, New Jersey : John Wiley & Sons, Inc., [2019] | Includes

    index. |

Identifiers: LCCN 2018034186 (print) | LCCN 2018036060 (ebook) | ISBN

    9781119516361 (Adobe PDF) | ISBN 9781119516378 (ePub) | ISBN 9781119516330

    (hardcover)

Subjects: LCSH: Self-perception. | Self-realization.

Classification: LCC BF697.5.S43 (ebook) | LCC BF697.5.S43 M59 2019 (print) |

    DDC 155.2--dc23

LC record available at https://lccn.loc.gov/2018034186

10 9 8 7 6 5 4 3 2 1

Contents

Preface

Extraction: As it relates to making red wine, this is the process of pulling out the true essence of the grape to produce the finest possible wine. While the juice is generally colorless, the skin, seeds, and stems add character, vibrancy, and flavor nuance. With too little extraction, the wine lacks color and complexity – too much extraction and the wine can be self-indulgent, overbearing, and brusque.

My earliest clear memories from my childhood are of me walking in the woods with my dogs. I spent many of my days, when I was as young as six years old, wandering and pondering. Much of this fondness to disappear into the woods had to do with the challenges facing my mother. She was dealing with the mental anguish brought on by a life cocktail of an unplanned second era of parenthood, undiagnosed depression, and menopause. As a result, she developed unhealthy relationships with vodka, barbiturates, diet pills, and my father. And she was not a happy drunk. My coping mechanism was to vacate the premises in hopes that she would pass out by the time I returned.

I have long since forgiven my mom, realizing that I arrived at a bad time for her. This book is not about her – but as it is a book predicated on the notion of fully knowing oneself, her influence on me must be included. I think it is also important to point out that despite her struggles, she exists in me through many of the traits of which I am most proud. Within every cloud there is a silver lining and such, as they say. For one thing, she indirectly and unintentionally but effectively inspired my ability to engage in metacognition, a concept that is discussed at length in this book.

My initial companion on these childhood journeys among the trees was my dog, Long John; or, as my dad called him, Bird Brain, due to his odd habit of chasing birds out of our yard. Soon, we were blessed with the arrival of Red, the most loyal and well-trained canine member of our family. Unlike Long John, whose attention span was commensurate with his nickname, Red never left my side from the time I walked out of the house and into the woods until I would return home many hours later. Perhaps it had to do with Red's puppyhood.

Red was already an adult when we first met. Judging by his demeanor, training, and appearance, he had been well loved and cared for. He was a passenger in a car accident near my hometown of Greenup, Illinois. My mother was a news stringer for the local television and radio stations and would contact local authorities to get details of any story that the area media might be interested in. A car accident, particularly one in which there was a fatality, was a big story in a small community. When she contacted the Cumberland County sheriff's department, they informed her that the driver of the car had been killed. The other occupant was unharmed but emotionally shaken. The lucky survivor was Red.

Touched by his plight, my mom sent my dad to collect Red and bring him to our house, where we would keep him pending notification of the family. Red's next of kin was the brother of his travel companion. Because that brother lived in Hawaii, it would be nearly a week before the family could arrange to pick up Red. Within that week, he had endeared himself to our family in a way that no other dog had previously done.

I remember the incredible sadness I felt the evening that we waited for Red's "uncle" to pick him up. We lived at the end of Wylde Drive, a dead-end road that stopped at our house. Eventually, a pair of headlights approached our home. The car pulled into the driveway and my mother, father, and I looked at each other and at Red and began to cry. We waited for the knock on the door. And we waited.

After a few minutes, the car backed out of our driveway and drove away. No one ever showed up to claim Red. It was one of the happiest days of my childhood. For the next several years, I had a hiking buddy nonpareil. It is not hyperbole to say there was no other creature, human or otherwise, that I was closer to than Red during this time.

In many ways, this book and my life in general are the products of my mom, my dad, and Red. Without my mom, I would not have taken to the woods, spending countless hours contemplating the world and my place within it. She also contributed to my aptitude for public speaking, a reporter and entertainer in her own right. Without my dad, I would not have my sense of duty; he stayed with my mom for 53 years, allowing only her death to separate them. And without Red, I would not have felt the security to take those walks alone, to turn my attention deep inside myself and start the trek inward to discover my truth.

Many others would aid my odyssey: my lovely bride, my children, my sister, friends, co-workers, clients, and more than a few strangers. We are all shaped by those who cross our path. I am thankful for them all, regardless of the context of our intersection, because each has allowed me to learn more about me, to grow, to become the best me possible.

Still today, 50 years after those childhood experiences with Red, I am drawn to long hikes of solitude when I feel unsettled, out of alignment. Having moved from Illinois to Florida to

Colorado and, finally, to Walla Walla, Washington, this habit – my "wander ponders" – have remained a part of my life. After arriving in Washington State's wine country immersing myself in the wine industry, I have come to realize that I've been undertaking the human equivalent of what the wine world calls "extraction." I am learning how to express my essence as a human being to be the best person possible. It is an expedition that never ends, but never fails to fulfill. Just like a winemaker working with the grape to create the perfect expression in a bottle, we are rewarded when we endeavor to find and display our gift.

And, just like a winemaker, my muse was Red.

Acknowledgments

Despite my lifelong fascination (obsession?) with metacognition, reflection, and contemplation, writing this book reminded me of the many people who have shaped my life. Many of them are mentioned within this work, but far more are not. As the cliché goes, "there are too many to list here." But there are a few too important to not list.

My lovely bride, Lori, is my reason for being. You never stop astounding me as a person, a spouse, a mother, and a friend. I love you more than I thought it possible to love.

My daughter Brooke and son Slade have made me a better human being. You make me proud. I love you both and will forever do everything in my power to ensure that your life is good.

My sister provided a pivot point in my life when I needed it most. I love you, Sis!

In addition to those mentioned in the book, my enduring gratitude is extended to Nancy and Russ, Tom and Peggy, Bonnie, Debby, all my teachers – by profession and by chance and my many clients and seminar attendees from whom I have learned more than I have taught.

A special thank you to the best editors in the business, Christine Moore and Vicki Adang, for their encouragement and ability to gently point out my narrative clunkiness. In the words of Hemingway, "write drunk, edit sober."

For their unwavering canine support over the years, a shout-out to Long John, Heidi, Fannie Mae, Killer, Toots, Goofus, Pilgrim, Sparky, Martini, Rossi, Boone, and Bob – the latter laid on the couch in silence while I muttered the occasional profanity during the writing of this book.

Mom, thank you for what you gave me. It was more than you knew.

Finally, this book is dedicated to my two original mentors: my dad and Red. I cannot think of either of you without the seemingly impossible experience of smiling and crying, simultaneously. I can't think of a better lingering effect on someone.

THE
POWER
OF
understanding
YOURSELF

PART ONE
THE GRAPE

Chapter 1 Metacognition

The Process of Evaluating "The Juice"

> In vino veritas – In wine, there is truth.
>
> – *Pliny the Elder*

I miss libraries. Oh, I know that they're still around, but I don't visit them. I am hopeful that some people still do, because I love the concept of a library. It is a magical place, a place to go where you have access to information old and new to broaden your knowledge. You can do research in a quiet comfortable location. There is always that worn, leather chair in the corner that only you know about. It is there that you settle in to embark on a journey. The library offers an environment that is precious in today's world. It allows for the solitary pursuit of information. You sit among the product of the efforts of the greatest minds of our time with tangible evidence of their efforts in every direction. With more motivation than plan, you start looking for wisdom. Your research may take hours, even days. You will have to return repeatedly to this wonderful, quiet place full of resources to expand your understanding of something. To gain more knowledge, you will be required to have some – to think about what you already know, get up out of your comfy chair and go find information that will broaden that existing knowledge. You will gather a stack of books and return to your chair to pour over them for useful nuggets, sifting through the chaff of unimportant or unnecessary material in your quest for the meaningful. And with each new piece of data, a new pathway for further enlightenment will open.

Such is metacognition. The library is your own brain. And like the libraries of today, while we know it's around, we rarely step inside.

METACOGNITION VERSUS SELF-AWARENESS

Metacognition is the process of thinking about thinking. More importantly for our purposes, metacognition is thinking about how *you* think. And although that sounds like a pretty easy undertaking, consider the daunting task of walking into the Carnegie Library to do some research on a topic of which you have only a superficial understanding with the expectation that you will leave it with absolute expertise. Take quantum physics, for example. I have heard it described this way, "Quantum physics is not just harder than you think, it is harder than you can think." You might know a little about physics, but it's going to take a whole lotta trips to the library to learn quantum physics. In that way, metacognition is an entirely other level of self-awareness.

And here is where metacognition differs from mere self-awareness. Most people have some degree of self-awareness. Using the library metaphor, we can define self-awareness as the shallow knowledge that you possess about a subject upon visiting the first time. You may go to the library to research the wine varietal Cabernet Sauvignon, for example, with the knowledge that it is a grape used to make wine. Upon researching it, you would learn that Cabernet Sauvignon is the "offspring" of Cabernet Franc and Sauvignon Blanc; it is one of the noble grapes of Bordeaux and is considered the "King of wine grapes." This in turn creates pathways to explore, related to the "parents" of Cabernet Sauvignon, why it became popular in Bordeaux and how it spread in popularity around the world. Each of those rabbit holes of research will introduce more things to explore, and so on. It is in this way that metacognition serves as a metaphor for the pursuit down these rabbit holes. Self-awareness is simply realizing that you behave in certain consistent ways and patterns. Put another way, self-awareness is simply knowing how you behave, but not why. For example, maybe you have worked with a boss that liked to tease other people. These bosses would likely be self-aware that they did this. They may have even bragged about their ability to "burn" members of their team. The fact that these bosses know this about themselves has only modest value. Metacognition would require that they knew why they behaved this way; what happened in their lives to initiate this desire, what usefulness this behavior had to them, what value he gained from this teasing. Being accurately self-aware is useful, but hardly the destination for extracting Me – a process the mirrors the winemaker's efforts to pull the best of the grape into the wine. Metacognition is the tool that we as individuals use to pull the best of our essence into our own expression of humanity. A person who is engaged in metacognition is examining why their behaviors exist, what formed them, are they useful, how can they be changed if they are barriers to our full potential. We bring into the library the knowledge of our behaviors (self-awareness) so that we can then research the reasons for these behaviors and their contribution to our best selves (metacognition).

THINKING ABOUT OUR THOUGHTS

Most of us have never engaged in extensive metacognitive activities. Why? Pretty much the same reason we don't go into the library these days: we don't have to.

The funny thing about our brains is that they work quite effectively without supervision. Think about the patterns of your days. You have routines. You have lists. You have calendars. You have handheld electronic devices. You know where you are going, and the few times you don't, you have technology to assist you. Soon the car will drive you there by itself anyway. You work, you sleep, you do errands. If something unfamiliar pops up, you can Google your way to a resolution without having to learn any more than superficial information about the issue. Nearly our entire existence is akin to running a computer app.

It is not an exaggeration to state that many years – perhaps even entire lifetimes – can pass without individuals stopping and actively examining their own thought processes. For all I know, these people are completely content living their own version of Groundhog's Day. The library just isn't that important to them. I imagine they say to themselves, "Why do I need to go looking for a deeper understanding of myself when I am happy with things as they are?" Discovering their Me is not important to them; it might even be a bit unnerving. There's not a thing wrong with that, and good for them.

As for me, I am infinitely curious about my purpose, my "gift," and what I can do to make the best use of it. That probably makes me the more neurotic of these two types of people. Perhaps the "blissfully ignorant" have the better path – and that isn't meant to be derogatory or provocative. To live a life of superficial self-awareness and be quite content in doing so is, *literally*, being blissfully ignorant. I have often envied those people. This book is not for them. I doubt they would buy this book anyway, so they are not my audience. If you have accidentally bought this book or received it as a gift, feel comfortable stopping here and re-gifting this to someone who would be interested. It's all good.

However, many of us *do* long for a deeper understanding of ourselves. Are we special? I mean, everyone says "of course, you are special!" But how do we know? What makes us special? Am I using what makes me special to affect others; to impact the world for the better? If not, what do I need to change?

If we are lucky, we get 80 or so years in this existence. I don't know what comes next, if anything. That's a different book. I want to know what I should be doing with *this* existence. To discover that, you need to go to the library. You need to engage in metacognition.

There are other things that deter us from entering the library. Besides not feeling compelled, there are a lot of distractions. Imagine if right next to the library were all forms of other ways to occupy your time; options that were easier to navigate. Picture cafes and clothing stores, sporting events and televisions, places to work and people to talk to. Imagine that every moment was filled with something to watch, someplace to be, something to search, websites to check, things to buy, errands to run.

Wait – you don't have to imagine that. I just described everyone's life. That is precisely why both the real and the metacognition library are not busy.

When can I possibly fit in a trip to the library – which, by the way, can be inefficient, unproductive, and downright frustrating – when my day is already so full? Metacognition is rarely on any things-to-do lists, and it is the odd day that we are looking for items to *add* to our lists. It's hard to envision a to-do list that says, "clean house, shop for groceries, pay bills, pick up dry cleaning, engage in metacognition, take dog to vet, work out, get oil change."

Plus, imagine if that trip to the library turns out to be unpleasant? What if you found that there exists some information inside that makes you sad, angry or – the worst – disappointed in yourself? But guess what? You will. So *now* how likely is it that you would take the trip to the library, what with it being not entirely necessary, potentially unproductive, likely make you feel bad sometimes – *and* you don't have time for it anyway. I mean, it's not like you are looking to make more time in your life fruitlessly seeking parking spaces or getting a few more paper cuts. Metacognition is a lot like both of those activities sometimes.

CHOOSING TO EXTRACT ME

So, *why* take this trip into the library of your mind? Simple. Therein lies the content of Me. But you must find it. You must decide to visit this space. You must think about what you know, then get up and research what you know so that you can know more. All that noise that you experience each day, both important and not, can drown out Me. To find it, you must walk into that quiet library.

The good news is that it doesn't really have to take place in a library (although there are worse places to engage in metacognition). I do my metacognition while walking in the woods. I didn't realize all those years ago when I went on my wander ponders with Red that I was learning some valuable skills in how to extract Me. And the coolest part about that? Red was my librarian.

That makes me giggle.

Let me give you an example from the wine industry. Many years ago, I decided to enroll in the educational classes necessary to become a certified advanced sommelier. My decision to do so was to be able to more intelligently and critically assess wine and more fully appreciate all that it had to offer. A close second for reasons to take the classes was the prospect of drinking lots of cool wine. (Okay, so perhaps those two should be reversed.) Anyway, I was very excited about furthering my knowledge of the wine world.

However, it didn't take long once I started classes to realize that this would be a lot harder than I thought. There was a great deal of reading about history, understanding geography, and *terroir*. Of course, there is the examination of the different colors, smells, and tastes that can be found in wine. The whole thing was intellectually exhausting. By the way, *terroir* is a cork-dork term for the influence of the place on the wine. Wine begins in the vineyard and each vineyard has a unique soil, moisture, sun exposure, land aspect, and so forth. In so many ways, a wine is affected by its roots. Just like us.

I became incredibly frustrated by how hard it was to fully understand this delightful fluid. I spent hours looking at, smelling, sipping (and occasionally spitting) hundreds of glasses of wine to understand their origins, the winemaking decisions, the impact of the vintage, and all the complexities that existed in that little taste. Despite what you might think, it was *not* fun. In fact, it was miserable. *But*, after a couple of years of study, I had developed a much deeper understanding of wine in general and a far great passion and love for each glass I experienced. Now, I look at wine in a very different and deferential way. I recognize the magnitude of the accomplishment that exists within that glass. I savor it for what it is. Each glass of wine *is* special.

Metacognition is a lot like that.

YOUR COGNITIVE SCHEMAS MAKE YOU UNIQUE

So, we begin this journey with metacognition. And metacognition arises from the question, "Am I special?" The answer is yes, absolutely, without reservations, unequivocally … *yes*. Let me explain why I am so certain of that, and why you should believe it too.

First, I am not a motivational speaker. I know many, respect most of them, and certainly appreciate their value. But, I am not one. I am an entertaining educator on the stage and I endeavor to inspire learning in both directions between my audience and me. But I am also a product of my experiences: that rural upbringing with a problematic relationship with my mother, a caring but emotionally stoic father, witness to life's injustices like everyone else. Heck, my dad's most frequent response to my complaints as a kid was, "Cheer up, it gets worse." I do not believe that repeating simple affirmations or learning some life hacks can radically change your life. I don't believe that there is a convenient seven-step process to happiness and success. Life don't care. Like that famous YouTube video, life is the honey badger; it don't give a shit. As a result, we will experience pain, suffering, unfairness, bad luck, heartache, and failure. *But*, we are still special. Here's why.

Each of us has become what we are because of our experiences. We are born and spend the first few years of our lives doing, seeing, hearing, and learning things for the first time – forming cognitive schemas to allow us to make sense of these experiences, and determine how to behave and process future events. Think of cognitive schemas as the policies and procedures of your mind. You are born without much programing, so what you go through initiates the process of downloading your software. Even more interesting, no one can predict exactly how you write these schemas into your brain. Two people can be exposed to the same experience and create completely different schemas. If you don't think this is possible, grab a bottle of wine (preferably from Walla Walla Valley!), sit down with a sibling, and discuss your parents. Chances are you will have different opinions of each. The way we perceive our experiences is a distinctly personal and mysterious process.

If you take a moment to understand the full impact of that last paragraph, you will realize something very powerful. First, the way you think – the essence of Me – is created by both your experiences and the mysterious process of how you created the cognitive schema to define, process, and respond to them. Second, no one has been exposed to the collective database of experiences to which you have been exposed. Finally, even when you have had shared experiences with others, you will create different schemas than them; sometimes those differences will be subtle, sometimes radically different. So, the three tenets of metacognition are

1. Experiences create cognitive schemas.
2. Our experiences are unique to us.
3. No two people construct the same schema, even in identical experiences.

Therefore, your cognitive schemas – the policy manual of your mind and the basis of your essence – are unlike anyone who has ever lived, lives now, and will ever live in the future.

I cannot think of a more apt description of *special*. The question isn't "Am I special?" That is undeniably true. The question is "Do I know what *makes* me special, and am I using that gift?" That question is much harder because it will require you to answer many more questions, such as:

- Where do I begin in this metacognitive process of extracting Me?
- What are the elements of my essence?
- How do I use my gift?
- How will I know if I have truly found Me?
- Are there cognitive schemas that inhibit my gift?

There is one last insight that can easily be lost in this discussion. We have far more influence over our reality than we realize. Our entire perspective, the way we define our experiences, is the product of our own cognitive schemas. *We* installed them. Most likely, this took place when we were quite young, before the age of 22, as we were experiencing most things for the first time. But now, further down life's journey, we continue to use these same cognitive schemas – despite some radical differences in context.

Imagine you ran a business for 80 years and never changed any of the company's policies after the first 20 years. Sure, some of these policies will stand the test of time, but most of them will need to be evaluated, updated, changed, and even eliminated. New ones will almost definitely need to be installed. The decision to do that would be up to you, and you would make those choices in the best interest of the business. Similarly, while reading this book, you may well discover that there are things about you that you are not using to their full capacity. You may also identify personal attributes that are hindering your full development and impact. Just like the business executive who must make changes to achieve better performance, so must you for your own performance. The willingness to do that has a lot to do with your locus of control.

Chapter 2 Locus of Control

You Are the Winemaker

Wine makes a man more pleased with himself. I do not say it makes him more pleasing to others.

– Samuel Johnson

"Life is like stew."

Admittedly, this was an odd way to begin a conversation with a colleague seeking counsel from me – their human resources executive – about a problem at work. Those who had heard the story before, and there were many, knew that this was how I responded to individuals complaining about the petty annoyances that are common in our lives. In fact, I told the story so often that it became known simply as the "Stew Story." It usually followed an employee sharing a grievance about a coworker, a manager, or a customer. They were frustrated about an irritating behavior or an unexpected life circumstance that had complicated their day. Most of the time, our employee-relations manager, who was infinitely more patient with the process than me, handled these conversations. That was precisely why I had hired Dee Dee Bracewell – to protect the employees from me. I was a more directive counselor. Pity the poor employee who chose Dee Dee's day off to air their grievance. After they shared their concern about their schedule, I would begin.

"Life is like stew."

"Stew has broth and chunks of beef, carrots, celery, and potatoes. Life is the same. Most times you find yourself scooting through the broth … easy peazy. It's smooth sailing, moving through that broth. Then, all of a sudden and with no warning, you run into a carrot. Smack dab, full stop carrot collision. Now, it's not the carrot's fault. Carrots are part of stew. Everyone knows that. So, it doesn't make any sense to be *surprised* by the carrot. I mean, you were bound to run into one eventually since you know – everyone knows – there are carrots in stew. You can blame the carrot, but that's kind of silly since you knew it was going to be there. The carrot is just doing its thing. So, the question is not, 'Why did the carrot do this to me?' The carrot is part of the stew. And the question isn't 'Why did I hit the carrot?' No one gets through the stew without hitting a carrot, a potato, a piece of celery. No, the question is "What do I do now that I hit a carrot?'"

It was usually at this point in my story that the recipient would stand and say, "I think I'll just talk to Dee Dee about this tomorrow."

DELUSIONS, CONTROL, AND DISAPPOINTMENT

The story makes a point about locus of control. Since you are reading this book, I am assuming you have a legitimate desire to understand yourself. If that assumption is true, then it follows that you are doing so to enhance your life in some way. Perhaps you want to be happier or find your true calling. Maybe you are seeking a better professional fit or trying to enhance your self-esteem. No matter the motivation, there is one cognitive schema that will provide the foundation for achieving your goal and it is related to your locus of control.

We are all delusional. I have written that in all three of my books. Some of the delusions we manifest contribute to our success and happiness; others provide barriers to the same. For my money, the single most important cognitive orientation for constructing our best delusion is our locus of control. Imagine your entire perception of the world was filtered through one lens and that lens determines if you believe the control of your life resides inside or outside of you. Let me be clear, all of this is a delusion since no one can control how their life will turn out and life cannot control absolutely your experience (unless you let it). It doesn't matter how much you *try* to control life. In the famous words of Woody Allen, "If you want to make God laugh, tell him about your plans." So, yes, believing that you can control life is a delusion.

But, orienting yourself to believe that you can *impact* life, despite what happens to you, is not a delusion. That is an internal locus of control. An individual who has an internal locus of control takes the actions necessary to direct life back to the desired path. They still hit carrots, but they don't blame the carrot. They may say, "Damn, never saw that carrot coming," but they take responsibility for the choices they make that lead up to the impact and for the strategy for returning them to the broth.

One of my favorite interview questions is, "Tell me about a time you disappointed your boss." Without fail, the interviewee shifts in their seat, hems and haws for a few minutes and says, "Gosh, I can't really think of anything." Now, we both know that is a lie. When I ask for a show of hands from my seminar audiences of who has disappointed their boss, every single attendee's hand goes up. We both know that the interviewee has disappointed his or her boss. To make it clear that evasiveness won't suffice as an answer, I just sit there and look at the interviewee. The silence increases the pressure.

"I mean, everyone disappoints their boss at some point, right?" the interviewee offers gingerly. The interviewee is desperately hoping to be taken off the hot seat at this point, but

I remain silent. Eventually, the interviewee will cop to a mistake that resulted in the requested example. What they don't realize is that I have almost no interest in the actual situation (unless it involved a felony!). I care about how they frame the episode during our discussion. Do they blame the boss, a co-worker, a customer, the situation? Or, do they share what they learned from the mistake – and how they improved as a result? If it's the latter, that tells me they have an internal locus of control. (Or they had previously attended one of my seminars.)

I've found that people can be taught most things if they have a legitimate interest and the requisite aptitude. Talent, experience, and knowledge are certainly important to success. But given the choice of working with someone who has all those things and an external locus of control versus someone who possesses an internal locus of control and less talent, experience, and knowledge, I will choose the latter every time.

FINDING YOUR LOCUS OF CONTROL

You might wonder how to tell if you have an internal locus of control – which is a fair and important question. The truth is, like most things about ourselves, locus of control is not binary; that is, it's not just one slide switch, it is more than one switch. A person can display an internal locus of control professionally, but an external locus of control in their personal relationships. We all know of people who are incredible performers at work, but who go home to horrible marriages. So, how do I gauge my own locus of control? I recommend two approaches.

In my first book, *Live and Learn or Die Stupid*, I coined the term Demon Committee Meetings. These generally occur in the middle of the night and consist of a sleepless obsession over something that is bothering you. It might be a mistake you recently made, a task that you must do, an argument you just had; the agenda for a Demon Committee Meeting can be long and varied. You toss and turn, displaying what blues performers have long called a worried mind. I used to hate these sleep- robbing, stress-filled events. Eventually, however, I realized the value of Demon Committee Meetings. They are your mind's way of itemizing the life events that you are externalizing your locus of control.

When you find yourself obsessing over an issue – whether at 2:00 a.m., as is the case with me, or during the day – the first step is to write down a things-to-do action list. I keep a handwritten things-to-do list near me almost all the time. I'm old school, so the act of putting pen to paper provides me a physical outlet for the expulsion of the demons. But you can do this on your phone or other device, too. The key is to immediately convert the mind's obsession to a plan of action. By doing so, you are converting your orientation to the challenge from external to internal locus of control. Meeting adjourned.

Let me give you a personal example. Because of the popularity of my seminars, I am offered book deals before I write the book. Generally, an author would complete a manuscript and then shop it to publishers. Since my situation works in reverse, I am writing my book under a contractual agreement that includes deadlines. It feels a little like attending college classes in that you have a large project, like a thesis, due on a specific date. As a result, it is not unusual for me to obsess – at 2:00 a.m. – about my progress on my current book. If I lay there and worry, this Demon Committee Meeting can last hours, perhaps the rest of the night. *But,* if I get up and add, "write 2,000 words" on my daily to-do list, I immediately feel better. I might go further and add, "map out mileposts for book progress." Almost without fail, the Demon Committee Meeting will conclude and the demons disperse. By the way, even though you are reading the final version of this book, it is my current book as I am writing this, so, yes, I wrote this chapter after yet another Demon Committee Meeting. We are all a work in progress.

The simple act of taking responsibility for my stress triggers and generating even a simple plan of action reduced my duress. So – what is stressing you out? What life events, situations, or relationships have been included in your Demon Committee

Meeting agendas'? List them. Write each one down and then commit to taking an action on each one of them. That action must be something that you control and will follow through on. Doing this shifts your orientation to an internal locus of control. It also cancels the Demon Committee Meeting for the foreseeable future.

Consider, also, how you think of your life. If you tend to compartmentalize your life, say, work versus home, you may want to have separate action lists for each segment of your life. If you view your life in a holistic way, one action plan will work. The key is that you have a plan of attack for your life and that it reflects the way you think about it.

The second approach is a little harder and is a call back to the "life is like stew" lecture. Unhappy people often talk about the life events that have resulted in their dissatisfaction. They blame relationships, bosses, money, parents, health, or any number of other variables in this complicated soup of life. This way of thinking reflects an external locus of control perspective. It reminds me of an exchange I had with my father over a pair of Converse Chuck Taylor All-Star tennis shoes.

It was my freshman year of high school, and basketball season practice had just begun. The coach recommended we purchase the Chuck Taylor All-Star shoes, which were conveniently offered at a special price through the school (nice marketing, Converse!) Anyway, all the cool kids were buying them. I went home to my father – the World War II veteran, Great Depression era survivor.

"Dad, can I get a pair of the Converse Chuck Taylor All-Star tennis shoes?" I asked sheepishly.

"What's wrong with the tennis shoes you already have?" Dad replied.

"The basketball coach told us we should get these."

"Is he buying them?" Dad shot back. I knew this was a bad sign. Apparently, my father did not view the basketball coach as a critical product specifier to the same degree I did. So, I tried to appeal to the power of peer pressure.

"No. But, everyone else on the team is buying them."

"You know, son, I used to worry about my shoes until I met someone with no legs."

Sometimes I wish my dad had just said "No" instead of making everything into a damn learning opportunity. Anyway, given that I was 14 years old and feeling the dreadful dual influence of hormones and peer pressure, I was pissed. What didn't occur to me at the time was that I had enough money to pay for the shoes myself. I had that money because my father had insisted that I work at his store each summer starting at the age of 12 to avoid spending my free time in less productive activities. Given how I chose to spend my free times in my late teens, this was yet another striking example of his good judgment but that is another story. This was an easy fix if I simply made the choice to act. Instead, I was angry that my father wouldn't buy them for me. It is a small moment in a person's life, but analogous for so many bigger ones. I am not sure if my father had purposely intended to teach me about the value of internal locus of control, but he had.

We all have our struggles. I have yet to meet the individual that has lived very long without a substantial heartbreak, tragedy, or burden. We don't get to choose all that life will serve up to us. But we can choose how we respond to that offering. That is the important takeaway. Unfortunately, even those of us with the most well-developed internal locus of control can fall victim to some episodes of externalizing that control. As you read this, you may have been reminded of a few life events that have had a tremendous impact on you. Some of you may still harbor some resentment toward these events, people, or situations. You may believe that they forever altered your life.

You are right.

You are right because you continue to *allow them* that role. An external locus of control makes you a victim to life. An internal locus of control heals your life. If there are things in your past that you continue to allow to have power over you, you will never be able to extract your best self. So, spend some time taking inventory of the past. Are you the victim of past relationships or experiences? Have you forfeited your power by manifesting an external locus of control over some part of your life? If so, I urge you to develop a plan to correct these items. Take action. That action should be positive and loving both toward yourself and those that will be affected – but take action. You will never extract your best self otherwise. It is like making wine from diseased grapes. No amount of winemaking can overcome the flaws in the juice.

There will be exercises and assessments in the chapters that follow, all meant to be helpful tools to guide your extraction. My hope is that this book will aid your understanding of yourself. But, despite the very useful information that you will uncover in the work that follows, nothing will have a greater impact on your happiness than an internal locus of control.

In the back of the book is the Extracting Me Worksheet. As you progress through the extraction process, you will be encouraged to write your thoughts down so as to assemble all your work when done. In that worksheet is a section on internal locus of control. The purpose of this segment is to stimulate an immediate action to improve your internal locus of control skills. Here are the questions/statements from that section:

> Consider an example in your life that reflects your use of an external locus of control that contributed to stress. List it and ask yourself the following:

- Why have I chosen not to manifest an internal locus of control on this issue?
- If I were to commit to one action that might positively affect this situation, what would it be?
- Am I ready to do that? If not now, why?
- Upon taking an internal locus of control action, how did this situation change?
- Did this outcome reduce my stress? Improve the situation? Why or why not?

Stop reading and start thinking. It is time for some meta-cognition and reflection. Complete this part of the worksheet before moving on to the next chapter. This will require some action, too, so be sure to do what is necessary to complete this section before moving forward. Remember, an internal locus of control is an essential tool for self-exploration.

We make choices every day and these choices have impact. Ask yourself how your choices have led to the life that you have and what choices you will make to achieve the life you desire. If you are not prepared to take responsibility for both – your life now and the one you desire – then the rest of this book will have very little value.

The beautiful irony of an internal locus of control is that only you can develop it. It is your choice. Many studies have concluded that individuals with an internal locus of control are happier, healthier, more resilient, and generally perform better than individuals who have an external locus of control. It seems like an easy choice to me. Besides, the purchase of this book is nonrefundable.

Chapter 3 Alignment

From Vine to Bottle

Wine, wit, and wisdom.Wine enough to sharpen wit, Wit enough to give zest to wine, Wisdom enough to "shut down" at the right time.

– Anonymous

These next two chapters are extremely important, closely associated, and more than a little complicated. I will admit that I struggled to clearly articulate both their meaning and their value. The most important outcomes for the next chapters will be to understand how critical it is to have a well-defined and meaningful core ideology and a process for continually evaluating it. The path to each of these outcomes will be explained more fully in what follows, but let's define what a core ideology and a process for evaluating it mean.

The term *ideology* has received some negative connotation in recent years. It has been used to express myopic or prejudicial thought. Our usage has no such meaning. For the purposes of extracting Me, core ideology represents our personal beliefs, values, and desires. They are a product of life experiences (inputs) and expectations (outputs). Think of your core ideology as the map that connects your past to your future.

The process for connecting our past to our future is what we use to both discover our core ideology and evaluate its effectiveness. Just like with a map, we would like this connection to be direct, aligned. Aligning who we are with what we want to be provides us a clear path to achieving a desired future state. In industrial psychology, this is known as organizational development (O/D). We will use some organizational development theories to guide our work. After all, organizations are simply groups of people who are responding to inputs with a goal of specific outputs. In this regard, O/D psychology is a perfect place to learn about big concepts that can be applied to our own journey. Considering that we spend the bulk of our conscious time preparing for, performing at, and returning from our vocation, it is no wonder that work has such a potential to teach us things about ourselves. I am no exception. My own pursuit of alignment and a meaningful core ideology was hugely influenced by my career.

A Master of Education degree (MEd) in Global Human Resources Development is not much of a conversation starter at parties. Thank goodness that I received an Advanced Sommelier designation, or no one would speak with me at all. Anyway, alignment and core ideology can be best understood with some context and models that I learned in graduate school. To fully understand the analogy, indulge me while I explain how organizations work. Think of it as receiving bonus education on industrial/organizational psychology in a book about cognitive psychology – a sort of buy-one-get-one-free thing.

INPUTS AND OUTPUTS

Figure 3.1 illustrates what a perfectly aligned, healthy organization would look like on paper. It was inspired by the work of Thomas Cummings and Christopher Worley in their

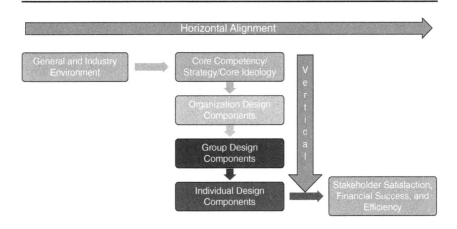

FIGURE 3.1   The concept of alignment in organizational development

book *Organization Development and Change*. On the top left of the diagram you see a box labeled General and Industry Environment. This refers to all the factors that impact an organization – economic considerations (market, customer demographics, competitors, employment rates, etc.), regulatory considerations (local, state, and federal laws, taxes, politics, permits, etc.), as well as any other issue influencing and/or affecting a company's viability. Think of all these components within the environment at inputs into the organization.

The bottom right of the chart shows the desired outputs. With rare exception, there are three specific elements of business outputs that represent the "scoreboard" for success: profitability, efficiency, and stakeholder satisfaction. Profitability seems obvious. Unless the company can generate a profit for ownership, its long-term prospects are dim. There are exceptions to this, but the most common construct of a company requires it to provide a return for ownership.

Efficiency is a far trickier metric. As markets fluctuate, revenues often take a crooked path upward. Rare is the organization that experiences consistent, uninterrupted revenue growth. Having run my own business for 23 years, I have experienced the tech bubble burst, 9/11, and the Great Recession to name just the ugliest of the economic ebbs and flows over that period. Efficiency in organizational development – as it relates to my model – is the ability to withstand changes in revenues brought about by market pressures and remain profitable. Many companies experience profitability that reflects the fruits of a robust market only to become unprofitable when that market becomes soft. I witnessed this repeatedly among my clients. The best companies could maintain solid profitability after the drastic economic downturn in 2008. Others did not.

Stakeholder satisfaction represents the three-legged stool of the human element of business. For an organization to remain healthy and high performing, three entities must be satisfied with their experience: ownership, customers, and employees. One of the most basic truths about human nature is that behavior breeds behavior. It is nearly impossible for a person to continually treat others well if they are not satisfied with the way they are treated. In this way, behavior is very much like a viral infection. Happiness begets happiness; misery begets misery. If owners are not happy, soon employees are not happy. If employees are not happy, soon customers are not happy. And if customers are not happy, soon owners are not happy. All three must be satisfied.

HORIZONTAL ALIGNMENT

A business, then, is a sort of living entity that successfully receives environmental inputs of and generates the outputs of profitability, efficiency, and stakeholder satisfaction. The first key to doing so successfully is to achieve "horizontal alignment," shown at the top of Figure 3.1. Horizontal alignment requires identifying a core ideology for your organization that responds to the general and industry environment and propels profitability, efficiency, and stakeholder satisfaction. A core ideology includes a vision for the future of the organization and a mission for what you promote as key to your success. Let's examine each of those components of a core ideology using a metaphor that most of us can relate to: planning a vacation. After all, a vacation is a great example of moving from an undesirable current state to a desired future state.

A *vision* is a desired future state for the organization. Think of this as selecting the destination for your vacation. Just as it relates to a business, one would typically imagine the vacation location to be an improvement over the current circumstances. There are two moments when a business focuses on a vision: at its inception, and at a strategic moment in a business's lifetime when it becomes aware of the need for a new direction. The latter of these two moments will be repeated many times for a successful business since the general and industry environment (inputs) can change often. For example, when I started my own business, my plan was to provide training resources to small and medium-sized organizations as an external human resources development partner. After a couple of years, it became clear to me that the industry environment/market was more robust for keynote speakers and conference breakout facilitators. I developed programs that worked more effectively as keynote speeches and 90-minute learning modules. I marketed to larger associations and companies. To achieve my desired outputs of stakeholder satisfaction, profitability, and efficiency, I adjusted my vision.

When I was working as a hospitality human resources executive in Orlando, we faced two environmental factors that required us to adjust our core ideology. One, the sudden growth in competition had put financial pressure on our yield management. In layman's terms, the room rates that we had been charging were historically higher than what many of the newer hotels were offering. Second, our hotel was quickly aging out of the fresh, new hotel market and into the established hotel market – that is, our hotel was looking a bit tired. Substantial capital upgrades were not scheduled in the immediate future, so we were faced with a competitive disadvantage as it related to the cosmetics of our property. We were not achieving our desired outputs. We were losing.

As is often the case when a company is experiencing a less than desirable current state of the organization, ownership was becoming unsatisfied. Referencing my earlier statement about behavior breeding behavior, I knew this dissatisfaction would soon create employee and, ultimately, customer dissatisfaction if not addressed. We were experiencing a textbook example of changes in our inputs creating a misalignment in our core ideology and, therefore, damaging our outputs. We lacked horizontal alignment. That's academic speak for "shit was hitting the fan." So, we endeavored on that frequent journey of corporate leadership: the retreat.

Our executive team went off property for three days to create a new vision, a desired future state, for the organization. Challenged by the twin obstacles of increased competition and no capital enhancements – and agreeing that reducing our room rates was not a viable strategy – we focused on competitive differentiators that required only a modest financial commitment. Immediately, we landed on the issue of service standards. We knew that service excellence was a potential advantage over the newer hotels in the area. We already had a system for training in place, but we had not integrated service excellence into our core ideology. So, our desired future state became "To provide the finest guest service in Central Florida – Five Diamond Service Excellence."

Back to the vacation analogy. Once you've chosen your vision – your vacation destination – the next decision will be, "In what vehicle will we travel?" That is the *mission*. Unlike the literal interpretation as it relates to a vacation, for a company, the mission is a singular and defining quality that the organization will leverage to achieve its vision. Vision is the desired future state, mission is the mechanism to move from where we are today to that state.

Our new vision of Five Diamond Service Excellence posed a very particular challenge. We had already promoted service excellence as an expectation of our employees. How were we going to change our current state by embracing a new mission that seemed to be rooted in our current state's culture? As we sat around the boardroom table, our president (Bob Stolz) shared a personal experience with service that became the basis for our mission. He related a recent trip to a restaurant at which he used valet parking for his car. After dinner, when the valet parker retrieved his vehicle, he quickly cleaned the windows with a squeegee. Bob was so impressed by this little extra special touch. He explained that most of our competitors provide great guest service. It's not enough to do everything the guest *expects*. He told us that Five Diamond Service Excellence was one step beyond the guest's expectation. "We need to do more than they expect; we need to squeegee them."

And then it happened. The entire executive team looked at each other. "That's it!" we exclaimed. We must invent a new word for service. A word that means something even greater than service excellence. We don't just serve our guests; we SQUEEG our guests. SQUEEG – Service Quality Unequaled, Efficiently and Enthusiastically Given. SQUEEG became our mission. We recognized and rewarded acts of SQUEEG by our employees. SQUEEG was the vehicle for achieving our vision. That shift in core ideology launched a new period of success at our hotel, in the face of daunting competition and limited capital investments. Such is the power of a clearly identified and articulated vision and mission.

In winemaking, the concept of alignment is a little different and probably even more applicable to a better understanding of ourselves. The input, the general environment (or *terroir*), is literal. It reflects the soil, the age of the vines, the aspect of the land, the precipitation, the sunshine, the temperature, and length of the growing season. Over decades, these factors combine to determine the types of grapes that will thrive – the fruit that will lend itself to producing the best wine. How one measures the "best" wine is also determined in large part by the outputs.

Some winemakers approach their craft like an artist steps to a canvass. The wine they will produce from the grapes will be an expression of their creative vision. For them, the output is a work of art and the financial measures are of only marginal importance. Other winemakers are pragmatists, considering more commercial metrics as critical outputs. The same is true about our own search for "Me." Knowing what you value as outputs will provide more clarity to your core ideology.

Finally, one must consider that life is not static. Our experiences continue to shape us as long as we live. It is true that as we age, each individual experience represents a smaller ratio to our total experiences and as such, tends to diminish their influence over us. But there are exceptions to this phenomenon. Just as companies can suddenly be faced with new competitors, technology, or regulations – and a winemaker must navigate an unusual vintage within their vineyards – a person may experience life-altering events. Sometimes these occur in the form of a singular, defining experience like marriage, parenthood, retirement, or tragedy. Other times they are the glacial-like developments that move without detection for years before we become aware of their existence.

As we move forward to applying the concept of alignment to our own personal core ideology, it is important to remember these points:

To understand ourselves, we must keep these three things in mind:

1. What are *the sum of inputs* that exist in our lives? We must understand the environment in which we developed and the one we find ourselves in today.
2. We must *identify what we value as outputs*. Do we measure of our success more on idealism or pragmatism? What role does money, happiness, spirituality, relationships, and other factors play in measuring Me?
3. Finally, we must remember that *both the inputs and outputs of our lives may evolve over time*. We will go through periods where our own core ideologies may be altered, even just subtly, to maintain our alignment. Extracting Me, like winemaking and organizational development, is a continuous cycle of evaluation.

But enough of the I/O psychology and winemaking talk. Let's examine ourselves.

Chapter 4 Core Ideology

The Crush of Juice, Stems, Skins, and Seeds

In victory, you deserve Champagne. In defeat,
you need it!

– *Napoleon Bonaparte*

There are several exciting occasions when you live in wine country. There is the spring release, generally a coordinated weekend when nearly all the wineries in the area make available their new wines for public consumption. This event is repeated in the fall, when it is rather obviously called the fall release. The most exhilarating of all the moments for me, however, is the harvest. Although not a precise point on a calendar, it reflects a moment in time for all winemakers when the grapes are picked in the vineyard, transported to winery, and subjected to the crush. The crush generates the must – a mix of juice with the solid components of the grape like stems, seeds, and skins. It is the raw material from which wine is made.

The crush is an obvious metaphor for distilling one's core ideology. It occurs after the grapes have been picked and sorted, so many of the inputs have been firmly established. It occurs before the grapes have been converted to wine, and have therefore not yet been linked to the outputs. The crush reflects the first big connection of inputs and outputs. It is the core ideology of winemaking. It is here and in the execution that follows that we will determine if we are indeed aligned.

As we explored in Chapter 3, an understanding of the concept of horizontal alignment in organizational psychology lends itself to self-discovery. We can map our lives out on paper in a manner very similar to the organizational chart at the beginning of that chapter. As adults, we find ourselves existing within a general environment, one that contains financial, relational, cultural components in addition to all manner of individual forces. We have considerations related to our health, geography, living arrangements – all of which are inputs affecting our lives, but not controlling them if we so choose.

In winemaking, we are extracting the best essence of the grape into the bottle of wine. This also means being mindful of those qualities that might detract from alignment. As humans, we are a collection of many characteristics. I happen to think that we are good at our core. But I also know that we all have attributes that can detract from being our best Me. Crush begins a process during which the winemaker makes many decisions about achieving desired outputs. These include identifying just the right number of components that, if applied too often or in too great a ratio, might misalign the wine. And so it is with us. A journey of extracting Me requires awareness of all our qualities, not just those of which we are most proud.

It is helpful to have at least a cursory understanding of cognitive development to truly explore the three most important questions along the path to extracting Me. These questions are:

1. Who am I?
2. Why am I who I am?
3. What can I do to be who I wish to be authentically?

For the purposes of this book, the answers to all these questions are reflected in the cognitive function of the brain. There are those people whose physical characteristics play a large role in how they perceive themselves. That is a different book. As such, for the purposes of answering those three questions, it is helpful to explore our own cognitive development. And the path from birth to adulthood as it relates to our cognitive development generally intersects with the work of psychologist Jean Piaget.

Piaget is most well known for organizing cognitive development into four age-associated stages culminating with the formal operational stage. It is not my intent with this book to explain, endorse, or criticize Piaget's work. However, there is no doubt that his work provided an early framework for understanding how we think and how that molds our perception of ourselves within the context of a complicated environment. The most important realization for the purposes of our own self-discovery is the realization that our Me begins being formed at the earliest of ages, is most influenced in our youth, and continues to evolve as we age.

Each experience we have in life becomes a smaller element of the entire inventory of life events. It is for this reason – I believe – that it becomes harder for us to change as we age. I imagine our true self as something like concrete. It begins soupy and pliable and hardens over time. It takes great force to break it once it is fully formed. In this way, it is essential that we examine how we hardened to appreciate the shape that we have attained.

I believe we all benefit from examining our childhood. What did we enjoy doing? What types of games did we most often play? What adults served as role models to us and why? What are the earliest memories of recognizing the traits of others that we most wanted to emulate? The answers to these questions offer important clues to how we formed our own core ideology as we entered adulthood. And while these continue to evolve after Piaget's final stage (postformal thinking), the influence of our environment during childhood remains strong. And if you desire to change that influence for some reason, you must first understand that it exists and why.

EXAMINING INPUTS

As in organizational development, our personal development begins with an understanding of inputs: the general environment within which we exist. Ask yourself these questions about your life. Examine the experiences, relationships, and activities that shaped your cognition. What do those things mean as they relate to how you think, what you prioritize, who you are? As we cobble together a true definition of Me, we must examine all aspects of how Me developed. Let's do that in a formal way. Here are some questions that you might ask yourself to understand your inputs. Feel free to let any and all these questions lead you down other paths of metacognition. Write your answers down. Repeat this exercise often. Contemplate what it means and how they relate to who you are today. By the way, this is an exercise in deep self-examination, so be prepared for some visceral emotional reactions. It's all good.

- In what ways did my parents contribute to who I am today? Siblings? Friends?
- What memorable childhood events or experiences have had a lasting impact on me?
- What successes in my past have made me the proudest? Why?
- What failures have I experienced that left a lasting impression? Why?
- What individuals have served as mentors to me and why?
- What characteristics in others are most inspiring to me? Why?
- What characteristics in others irritate me the most? Why?
- What are my happiest memories?
- What are my saddest memories?
- If I could change one thing about my childhood, what would it be? Why?

To stimulate the process here, let me share an example of an individual who had a huge influence to me as a mentor.

My human resources development career began at Marshall Field's in Chicago. Marshall Field's was a large, regional upscale department store chain primarily in the Midwest. Working at Marshall Field's was my first experience in a corporate setting. I began as the training manager at the Old Orchard store in Skokie, Illinois. Within a year, I was promoted to the same role at the flagship store on State Street in downtown Chicago. The boy from little old Greenup, Illinois, population 1,500 was now in an office on the 13th floor in the third-largest city in the United States. There were more people shopping and working in this store than lived in my hometown. I was overwhelmed.

My responsibilities were to ensure all the employees, over 1,000, were properly trained on the point-of-sale system, understood the company policies and procedures, and were prepared to deliver exceptional customer service for which Marshall Field's was legendary. I still remember taking the train into the city, walking with the multitudes, and making my way to the human resources office for my first day of work. My boss was Susan Wally. Susan Wally changed my life.

Susan Wally was six feet tall before slipping on the four-inch heels that she wore every day. Her hair was fiery red and she wore glasses that would have made Elton John pause. Her fashion sense steered toward neon. She had an easy laugh that came in one size, like everything else about her. Susan was a presence. The irony in all this was that Susan was the Director of Human Resources, typically a role filled by the most conservative, image-conscious professionals. But Susan was certainly not conservative.

I arrived in Susan's kingdom, and it truly was, with a reputation as a hardworking, compliant, smart, and reliable over-achiever. I had shown great promise as a presenter but was careful to stick to the corporate endorsed scripting, timing, and objectives. I was a worker bee. Susan did not place a high value on worker bees. What she wanted was some panache. To say that Susan liked to think outside the box would insinuate that she had any awareness of the existence of boxes and would therefore be inaccurate. Initially, I was petrified of Susan because she wanted things from me that I had never utilized in myself. She wanted me to spread my wings, take chances ... let my freak flag fly. "This is State Street, Dave. We don't comply, we create. We don't follow them, they follow us." Susan would say this about the corporate human resources people who were housed only one floor above us in the place we store personnel would call "the ivory tower," with a hiss.

So, I started to dip my toe in the notion of cutting loose. Initially, this was to win favor with Susan, but very soon I realized I liked going rogue. I became more outspoken. I challenged ideas, approaches, even people. My classes became more fun and, perhaps, a bit more unpredictable. Susan Wally tapped into my inner weirdo and I liked it. To this day, my style as a presenter owes its origins to the influence of Susan Wally. True to form, Susan entered my life like a comet and left it the same way. After being promoted to Director of Human Resources at another store and eventually leaving Marshall Field's, I lost track of Susan. Many times I have tried to track her down to let her know how much she influenced me, but to no avail. If you are reading this book, Susan, I would love to hear from you.

Susan was instrumental in helping me realize my own form of creativity. She gave me confidence to take chances and provided the work environment I needed to "find my voice." My educational philosophy of "laugh and learn" was in large part a result of this period in my life. That is what an input looks like when you examine your own life. Take some time now and complete the Inputs section of the Extracting Me Worksheet.

ASSESSING YOUR DESIRED OUTPUTS

Inputs –as they relate to an organization – are only one side of the equation. We also have desired outputs, which are arguably even more important to identifying your individual core ideology, since they represent how you *want* your life to be measured. In fact, a truly internal locus of control orientation would dictate that it is the outputs, not the inputs that determine the person. Most of our life, experiences as a child – particularly the first three stages of Jean Piaget's model, which occur before the age of 12 – were dictated to us. As adults, it is essential that we assess the outputs we aspire to in life and confront the likelihood that we possess some cognitive schemas, created in response to experiences in childhood, that run contrary to those desires.

That is the true value of horizontal alignment in both organizational and personal development. How do we connect the life experiences that have shaped us with the life results that we desire? That connection is our core ideology.

Outputs may well be like the ones I listed for a company, with just a bit of reshaping. Profitability becomes financial goals, efficiency becomes simplicity/well-being, and stakeholder satisfaction becomes our personal happiness and the health of our relationships. How do we exist within the environment we are in and experience a life that achieves our desire for a certain level of wealth, simplicity, physical and mental well-being, personal happiness, and relationship health? Of course, you can alter those outputs if you feel your life scoreboard should have different metrics. I think financial, physical, mental, and relationship health combined with personal happiness and spiritual satisfaction is a damn fine existence. It sure works for me.

When I was working in the corporate world, I was not experiencing all my desired outputs. My financial goals were okay, if not stellar, but my life was not simple, my well-being was not properly cared for, my relationships were stretched thin due to the time commitment – and I was not happy. As for spiritual issues, I ignored that completely. So, my scoreboard indicated that I was losing. And just like when an organization realizes that their core ideology is not successfully converting inputs to desired outputs, I needed to change.

First, I needed to determine: What was my desired future state? What was my vision? The reason I entered and stayed in Human Resources was that I liked to teach, develop, coach, and enhance others. With each promotion in my career, I seemed to be doing less of those things and more policy development, litigation defense, and long- term strategic consulting. It's not that I didn't like any of that; it just wasn't where I found my joy. Work had become unfulfilling, sometimes even just plain drudgery. I needed to revisit my core ideology so that I could align myself with my environment and desired outputs. But each day was so filled with activity, so exhausting and busy, that I never seemed to have time to engage in any meaningful self-evaluation.

Had I taken the time to explore my inputs, my general environment, I would have recognized the misalignment. Among the joys of my youth was helping others, presenting, coaching, and teaching. The models and mentors that I had as a child were those caring teachers who took genuine pleasure in helping me understand something new, or a coach that instructed in a manner that revealed their love of improving others. Even at play, I enjoyed constructing new games and experimenting with their effectiveness.

One particular memory from my youth has been deeply imprinted on me and seems like an especially important element of my cognitive development. As it is with many of the best memories of our youth, it revolved around summer vacation. I was fortunate that my best friend, Dennis, lived just up the street from me, not more than a half mile away. Not that any point in a town of 1,500 people is particularly far away, but Dennis's house being so close meant we spent almost every day together in the summer. Dennis's mom, Alice, became my surrogate mother. Dennis and I would spend the summer thinking of ways to occupy our time. I never fancied myself a nostalgic person, but I do miss those days of having to figure out what to do. This was the late 1960s/early 1970s, before video games and Internet access. Heck, we only had three television stations. So most of our entertainment revolved around riding our bikes around town or finding ways to play sports: baseball, football, and basketball. When it rained, we were left to our own creative devices to figure out a way to do the latter.

We must have had a dozen ways to play baseball inside on those inclement weather days. Some were as simple as tossing a coin to determine the winners and losers of every game on the schedule for the year. Our greatest resource was the current copy of Street's and Smith's Baseball Yearbook. Inside was a treasure trove of player information, statistics, and team schedules. We would diligently follow that schedule, flipping a coin to determine the winner of each game for 24 teams over a 162-game schedule. Considering each game involved two teams and allowing for the playoffs, I calculate that to be just shy of 2,000 coin flips. Imagine that level of monotony in today's world.

Most of our activities, however, were the result of days' worth of planning, creating, discussing, and educating. The primary motivation for this was the faint knowledge of Strat-O-Matic baseball. Strat-O-Matic ran ads in Street's and Smith's Baseball Yearbook and it was our fantasy. But, just like those Converse Chuck Taylor All Star tennis shoes, it was not a purchase my Dad was keen on. Unfortunately, I had not yet started working either. So, we developed our own baseball card game using index cards and dice. With only the current copy of Street's and Smith's Baseball Yearbook, we would produce an index card for each player on each team with a table reflecting six columns and eleven rows. In each of these 66 slots on the table, we would place a symbol for outs, walks, single, double, triple and home run. We would test the results so that the dice rolls (one die for the column, two dice for the row) generate statistics that were reflective of the players' actual performance. It wasn't perfect; as I remember one season Sandy Alomar, Sr. won the home run title despite never hitting more than four in a season in his actual career. (It may have something to do with me being a fan of Sandy Alomar.)

The point is, it seems obvious in reflection that I had a love of creating, discussing, and educating. My previous book and most popular seminar, *The Power of Understanding People*, contains all these elements. It is little wonder why this program became so crucial to my success and happiness. It was in complete alignment with my life inputs and desired outputs. It reflects my core ideology.

But, 20 years after my boyhood environment and before the creation of *The Power of Understanding People*, I sat in a corporate office – miserable. I was indeed unaware of just how miserable I was, since most people around me were similarly miserable. Maybe that is why misery loves company. It can hide.

Then, it happened.

I can't say that I am entirely proud of this episode in my career. In fact, it occurred as a direct result of some small amount of insubordination borne out of extreme duress. In retrospect, it was clear that I was in the end stage of a nearly five-year slow burn toward complete meltdown. I had been unhappy for a while. It's funny how unhappiness can become so prevalent in your life that you don't even recognize it after a while. It just becomes part of your current state; it certainly isn't desired, but it is almost invisible. In fact, I think many of us are experiencing a current state in which unhappiness is just part of it. And *that* makes me sad.

Anyway, it was in the unhappy current state that I sat in one of our weekly leadership meetings. These meetings operated like a sort of briefing for our president as each of us took turns updating our peers and our boss on the developments within our departments and fielding questions from each other. As the meeting stretched on (and on, and on), I became more frustrated with discussion. Finally, the president turned to me with a simple question.

"When are we going to schedule the annual employee opinion survey?" he asked.

"Why bother, we don't care," I responded.

Have you ever said something that gets about two feet out of your mouth before your brain has approved its delivery? I swear I could hear the collective "GULP" of each of my peers in impressively choreographed unity. Inside my head, a little voice said, "Oh no. That's gonna play poorly."

It is a testament to my boss's leadership skills that he didn't respond. I fully expected and deserved it. But Bob merely suggested that we meet on the topic privately. Part of me thought I should bring my personal belongings with me to that meeting.

Although I worried that I had gravely overstepped my position with the remark, another part of me recognized just how out of alignment I had become. This was not behavior consistent with *me*. Something needed to change. I had an epiphany. By the next day, I had the core ideology of the Leadership Difference, Inc. – my company.

The most amazing thing about making a commitment to identifying your core ideology is that it is so easy. It didn't take me more than an hour to realize what needed to change. So much of my work was spent in pursuits that, at their very essence, were not having a positive effect on others. That was the source of my misalignment. For me to connect my environment – my life – with the outputs that I aspired to have, I needed a simple but radical shift. I wanted to positively impact the life of each person with whom I came in contact, just as those teachers and coaches who had done so for me. And just like that, I had my desired future state: my vision.

But *how* would I do this? How would I positively affect the life of each person with whom I came in contact? Throughout my career, I always felt the highest levels of self-efficacy when in front of an audience – teaching, laughing, learning. As a child, I loved to create and educate people using fun. I was always something of the class clown. I wanted to share thought-provoking perspectives on life and work through humor. I wanted to laugh and learn! BOOM! My mission: "Laugh and Learn!"

And so, in 1995, at the age of 34, I left an executive position in hospitality and started my own company with those elements of a core ideology. Twenty-three years later, I am still traveling the world delivering those thought-provoking perspectives on life and work through humor. Although my business strategies may change, my core ideology has remained constant – because today, just as then, it is aligned with my environment and my desired outputs. Thus is the power of alignment. However, although my professional core ideology has remained virtually unchanged, my personal core ideology does continually shift ever so subtly. Again, the power of alignment.

IDENTIFYING YOUR CORE IDEOLOGY

"But what about me?" you may be asking. "How do I identify *my* core ideology?" Time for some more metacognition. Start by asking yourself the questions posed earlier in this chapter. What gave me joy as a child? Who most impressed me growing up? How did I like to spend my time? Many of the clues to our core ideology can be discovered by reexamining those experiences that positively shaped us.

There are also a few exercises that can help you form your core ideology. I developed one that has been very useful for guiding my own personal core ideology over the years. Let's work through it.

Below is a list of personal attributes that can become the cornerstone for your core ideology. This is hardly comprehensive, and you can add to the list by searching the Internet (Google "core values") or supplying your own. The point of this exercise is for you to think about Me. What gives Me joy. What fills Me with a sense of purpose. What aligns Me with my environment.

As life would have it, I am writing this chapter during March Madness and it is likely for this reason that my approach to this list reflects the style of elimination of the NCAA College Basketball Tournament. So, begin by cutting this list of 50 items by half, then by half again. Keep going until you get to 10 attributes that you think best describe you or that drive your aspirations:

- Family
- Health
- Wisdom
- Competitiveness
- Relationships
- Affection (Love)
- Cooperation
- Mediation

- Fame
- Achievement
- Appreciation
- Wealth
- Freedom
- Performing
- Empathy
- Integrity

- Inner harmony
- Creativity
- Helping others
- Personal development
- Love of country
- Nature
- Recognition
- Knowledge
- Independence
- Status
- Spirituality
- Religion
- Loyalty
- Adventure
- Teaching
- Economic security
- Pleasure

- Power
- Responsibility
- Order (stability)
- Solving problems
- Consistency
- Culture/ethnicity
- Political activism
- Social justice
- Physical appearance
- Excitement
- Physical labor
- Critiquing
- Fixing things
- Writing
- Playing games
- Research
- Fairness

As an example, here are the 10 attributes that I selected for me in no particular order:

- Family
- Health
- Loyalty
- Teaching
- Economic security

- Freedom
- Performing
- Inner harmony
- Social justice
- Helping others

Remember, you can add your own descriptors to the list if you like. You may also want to engage friends and family in this exercise as well, particularly if you are more extraverted. In fact, this can be a very cool exercise to do in a small group.

It is important to point out that just because an item doesn't make your top 10 doesn't mean it has no impact on you. I believe myself to be a very empathetic person, but empathy is not on my list. That is what makes this exercise deceptively challenging. You must consider what really *defines* you, not merely what qualities you possess.

Once you have narrowed your list to 10 items, it is likely that all these attributes play a significant role in your core ideology. However, I recommend that you narrow your focus just a little more. So, cut your list to the top five.

This will be hard.

Again, discussing this with loved ones can help you separate your aspirations and attributes from your actions. Actions are more reflective of your ideology than your aspirations – you know, the whole judge-a-man-by-his-deeds-not-his-words thing. For example, I aspire to impact social justice, but my actions – other than the occasional activism march or political post on social media – betrays that priority. Perhaps my core ideology will evolve to elevate this attribute in my future and thus convert aspirations to actions, but my current approach to life suggests that social justice is not among my top five. Sometimes other people can provide feedback about how your actions and aspirations differ. Be openminded; as they say, the truth hurts sometimes.

My top five settled as:

- Family happiness
- Economic security
- Teaching
- Freedom
- Helping others

What are yours? List them in the Outputs section of the Extracting Me Worksheet.

Are you surprised? Have they changed over the course of your life? Mine have. As little as 10 years ago, my longer list would have contained more elements related to achievement and competitiveness. In just the past five years, inner harmony and loyalty would probably have been on the short list. The point is that core ideology is not static. You must evaluate it at regular intervals to ensure that you are horizontally aligned as discussed in the previous chapter. As your life inputs and desired outputs change over time, so, too, will your core ideology. Some items may always help define it – family happiness and helping others have probably always been a part of my core ideology – whereas others will elevate and diminish based on what you are dealing with or what you are aspiring to.

The final two steps to this exercise will require some introspection. Although it can be useful to brainstorm with others, the final definition of your core ideology is a deeply personal undertaking. First, define each of the five attributes that you feel best describe what is important and true about you in your own words. Many of the characteristics appearing in the original list of 50 have different meanings to each person. For example, the word *spirituality* can mean a completely different thing for me than you.

So, write your definition for each of the five descriptors. The definition should be brief but specific to you. You may find that when you define one of your attributes, you include language from another characteristic that was on your list of 10 but did not make your list of five. That's perfectly fine.

Here are my definitions:

- **Family happiness** – To do what I can to promote a family experience that is loving, fulfilling, secure, and free of unnecessary hardship.
- **Economic security** – To have enough money to live a lifestyle that is comfortable and allows us to experience joy and contentment relative to our material needs.
- **Teaching** – To facilitate knowledge, awareness, and personal development in others while remaining open to new perspectives and information for myself.

- **Freedom** – To manage my life, my time and my effort in a manner that reflects my priorities independent of the demands and expectations of others.
- **Helping others** – To be a positive resource to those around me.

How would you define your five core values? Write these definitions for each core value on your Extracting Me Worksheet.

Once you have written those definitions, you have everything you need to write your own personal core ideology statement. Remember, my professional core ideology was "to positively affect the life of each person with whom I come in contact" using a "laugh and learn" style of teaching. It heartens me to realize how closely that aligns with my core values of teaching and helping others. Considering that ideology has consistently guided my success for the past 23 years, I would say that it has also aligned with my value of economic security and freedom, too. *And,* considering that my work keeps me on the road around 200 days a year, it probably has contributed to my family's happiness. (I kid, I kid.)

My personal core ideology would read like this:

To contribute to a loving, happy, and secure family while maintaining my freedom, economically and philosophically, to facilitate knowledge and transfer of learning for the purposes of being a positive and joyful influence on others.

What is your core ideology? Write your core ideology on your Extracting Me Worksheet.

Although the final product may be a simple paragraph, even just a sentence, the importance of articulating your core ideology cannot be overstated. It is what anchors you in life. It is what guides you and your journey. I have noticed that when I am feeling out of sorts or particularly stressed, it is almost always because I have strayed from my core ideology. It is a large part of Me.

Document your core ideology. Print a copy. Put it in a visible place. Refer to it often. Life is a noisy, confusing, and complicated experience within which we can lose our sense of self very easily. Your core ideology is the equivalent of a signpost on a long and isolated hiking trail. Heed it.

VERTICAL ALIGNMENT

One last thought on the concepts of alignment and core ideology. You will note that Figure 3.1 in Chapter 3 included "vertical alignment." In an organization, vertical alignment refers to each level of the organization, and each process contained within it must be aligned around the core ideology. That means that every policy, procedure, philosophy, behavior, evaluation, and expectation should align with the organizational beliefs. The words on a poster in the employee cafeteria espousing noble values and practices are worthless if they aren't reflected in the daily operations of the business. There is no credibility in a company that says one thing and does another.

The same is true about us. You have just spent meaningful time in a pursuit of your core ideology. You examined the life experiences that shaped you and the desired future state to which you aspire. You created your map for that journey. All of that is meaningless if your core ideology is not reflected in all aspects of your life. We all know people who behave one way in their professional roles and another in their personal life. For your core ideology to have the desired impact on your life, it must be adopted wholly, not in part. That is the meaning of vertical alignment as it relates to personal development.

We all can struggle or temporarily lose our way and get out of alignment. For me, when I focus too much on my own needs, I can inadvertently betray my core ideology. If I pursue my own impulses without being mindful of the impact it has on the life of another, I am fundamentally misaligned with my core ideology. The result is very similar to a misaligned organization. I do not reach my full potential. Episodes like this will happen, but the more specifically we define our core ideology and take care to remain aligned, the better we become, thus, the importance of both alignment and core ideology. Think of core ideology as the person you both are and continue to aspire to be despite changes in life inputs. Horizontal alignment is identifying that core ideology that connects from where you came to the desired future state (or even current state is you have arrived, so to speak). Vertical alignment is about ensuring that all your behavior, in all parts of your life, aligns with that core ideology. The analogy in the wine world would be that a winemaker will apply a core ideology to the making of his wine that responds to the inputs to achieve the desired outputs. That same core ideology will be applied to every type of wine that the winemaker makes. He does not alter his core ideology for each wine.

When successful winemakers examine the fresh harvest from the vine, they do so through the lens of ideology. They have a clear philosophy for converting the bountiful clusters of fruit during the crush into an amazing expression of the grape. The crush creates the must. It is from this concoction that the wine will be created. Just like the bitter components of the grape – stems and seeds – contribute to the character of the wine, we are shaped by both our good and bitter experiences. The crush begins the execution of that ideology, the input of the process, transforming the incoming grape into a desired final output – an amazing wine. All of their efforts are aligned on that final output. And they do it with their individual panache, their own unique style.

PART TWO
THE STYLE

Chapter 5 What's My Style?
Shades of Me

If you like it, drink it. If you don't like it, drink it fast!

— *Dave Mitchell before every wine-tasting event*

In the world of winemaking, you will often hear the term *style*. It most often relates to "new world" – a style of winemaking that emphasizes the flavor of the fruit (grape) – or "old world," a style of winemaking that emphasizes the sense of place from where the wine comes (*terroir*). The same varietal of wine, say, Cabernet Sauvignon, can be extracted in very different ways based on the style of winemaking. The same is true about people.

There are few elements of our self that are more intriguing to us than our interactive style. By the time we reach adulthood, nearly every one of us has completed some style inventory like the MBTI, DISC, True Colors, and so on. We have been told we are an INFJ – an introverted intuitive feeling judger, or a High D with a corporate hook C, or a "green who gets red under pressure." My previous book, *The Power of Understanding People*, focused exclusively on style. And although it would *appear* to be shameless self-promotion, I do recommend picking up a copy of that book. It will help guide you through a more thorough explanation of the concept of interactive style and allow you to discover a Hollywood movie character description of the way you interact with the world and other people. (Yes, my assessment reports in Hollywood movie characters – which I happen to think is a whole lot more fun than a letter or color.)

I know not everyone wants to go buy another book. And for those who have read *The Power of Understanding People*, I don't want to "till old soil," as they say. The last book focused on how to better understand and relate to other people; this book is directed inward. So, while there may be a little review for anyone who has already read *The Power of Understanding People*, this chapter will offer both a deeper and broader examination of interactive style as it relates to understanding yourself. For those who read *The Power of Understanding People*, I strongly recommend reviewing this information for two reasons. You will discover more about your style strengths, opportunities, and blind spots. After all, it has been five years since I wrote that book and I have gotten smarter since then. Further, the application is different this time—and, it is possible for people to evolve into different styles over time. For those reasons, it can be beneficial to you to start the process again. I have endeavored to limit any unnecessary redundancy.

To begin, you will need to complete the assessment from *The Power of Understanding People*. As an educator, I want to make this easy, so I have included that assessment in this book. Please read the directions carefully and keep this one very important caveat in mind: it is essential that you are *honest with yourself* when you complete the assessment. There are no right or wrong answers. Your values and character are not being evaluated. Move quickly through the assessment. When you are done, total each of the four columns. To make sure you have done the assessment correctly, total each of the four column totals. That number must be 120. If your four column totals don't add up to 120, something is wrong. Reread the instructions and try again. If you still don't get 120, sheepishly invite a friend with better math skills to look at your assessment.

The Power of Understanding People

Name_____ Date_____

Below, there are 12 sections, each with four statements labeled "a," "b," "c," and "d." After you read statements a, b, c, and d, choose the one that you find most appealing and put a "1" in the box next to the letter that matches that statement; put a "2" in the box of the statement you find next most appealing; a "3" in the next; and a "4" in the one you find least appealing.

---

a. Your favorite restaurant or vacation spot
b. Family and/or friends
c. A new place or situation
d. A competitive and/or learning situation   a. ☐2   b. ☐1   c. ☐4   d. ☐3

---

a. A well-structured company
b. A people-oriented company
c. A creative company
d. A fast-growing company   a. ☐1   b. ☐4   c. ☐3   d. ☐2

---

a. A job or project that is well organized
b. A job or project that benefits others
c. A job or project that is different and exciting
d. A job or project that is mentally stimulating   a. ☐2   b. ☐1   c. ☐3   d. ☐4

---

a. A dependable relationship
b. A meaningful relationship
c. An exciting relationship
d. A respect-based relationship   a. ☐4   b. ☐3   c. ☐1   d. ☐2

---

a. Rewards based on quality
b. Rewards based on teamwork
c. Rewards based upon originality of ideas
d. Rewards based upon merit and achievement   a. ☐1   b. ☐4   c. ☐2   d. ☐3

---

a. Feeling secure
b. Being appreciated
c. Something interesting
d. Being independent   a. ☐2   b. ☐1   c. ☐4   d. ☐3

---

a. An experience that delivered on promise
b. A moving emotional experience
c. Something unexpected and interesting
d. A winning experience

a. [2] b. [3] c. [4] d. [1]

a. A task that one can see or touch
b. A task that makes one feel good
c. A task that calls upon one's imagination
d. A task that requires logical reasoning

a. [4] b. [1] c. [2] d. [3]

a. Consistent work
b. Harmonious work
c. Changing work
d. Efficient work

a. [2] b. [4] c. [3] d. [1]

a. Being accurate
b. Being compassionate
c. Being innovative
d. Being productive

a. [2] b. [3] c. [4] d. [1]

a. A meeting to discuss details
b. A meeting to discuss feelings
c. A meeting to discuss ideas
d. A meeting to discuss results

a. [3] b. [1] c. [2] d. [4]

a. Knowing the directions
b. Working with a great team
c. Discovering something new
d. Being done with a project

a. [1] b. [2] c. [4] d. [3]

TOTAL   a [26] b [23] c [36] d [30]

When you are through ranking the items, add up all the numbers in the "a" column and total them at the bottom of the column. Then do the same for the "b," "c," and "d" columns. Finally, add the four column totals. That number must be 120.

The four columns of this assessment correspond to the four interactive styles described in *The Power of Understanding People*. For a full understanding of how these style impact leadership, selling, customer service and interpersonal relationship, I recommend checking that book out. But for extracting Me, we will explore what your scores say about *you*. Remember, this assessment is meant as a tool for metacognition and self-exploration. It is not comprehensive. Let it guide your process but feel free to expand beyond what the results may suggest when you feel it is appropriate.

UNDERSTANDING INTERACTIVE STYLE

You might be wondering, What is *interactive style,* anyway? Well, our minds are very complicated. We have learned to think the way we do based on millions of life experiences that we have amassed. As a result, we have created an approach to cognition that is uniquely ours – our own delusion, if you will. But, we still have an innate need to connect with each other. We yearn for companionship and connectedness to others. How does a uniquely delusional creature connect with others of its species? There must be ties that bind – or as Carl Jung would say, "a collective unconscious." Our interactive styles are a form of this. They are a unifying cognitive element in a sea of individuality. They allow us to effectively communicate, build relationships, and understand one another. Just as the individual grapes hang together in a cluster in the vineyard, so, too, do we as humans.

My model consists of four interactive style schemas: Romantic, Warrior, Expert and Mastermind. Each reflects a different sensitivity to the world. Each communicates in a slightly different way. Each corresponds to its own behavioral cues. Each has its own strengths and vulnerabilities. And while we all possess all four of these interactive style schemas, understanding your own *preferences* can help you better understand yourself.

The style we prefer the most provides the easier vehicle for connecting with others (as reflected by the thickest connection).

Our secondary preference provides a comfortable alternative when our primary preference is less effective within the dynamic we find ourselves. It also adds breadth and complexity to our primary preference. The tertiary style is more challenging for us to use and offers a wonderful opportunity for personal development. Although its natural impact may be subtle, it can be developed to broaden our interactive dexterity. The least preferred style (quaternary preference) often reflects our most vulnerable context – the blind spot when dealing with others. Understanding the strengths and vulnerabilities relative to how we use, or don't use, each of the four style preferences is essential to metacognition.

An examination of style provides useful information on recognizing your natural style strengths. This activity serves to educate you on how you can stretch yourself, develop your skills, expand your strengths, and be more aware of potential limitations and blind spots as they relate to communication and relationships. It is essential to extracting Me. Let's figure out what your scores mean.

The lower your score, the higher your preference is for that style. That is important to keep straight, since we often associate larger numbers with greater weight. However, in the case of this assessment, low scores tell us our sensitivities; high scores tell us our blind spots. Before we get into the meaning of each column, let's put some thought into the distribution of your preferences. I have found that the pattern of the totals is a meaningful metric when engaged in metacognition. Regardless of which column is your lowest and which is your highest, the *range* of your numbers is important. These ranges fall into three categories: dynamic, nuanced, and common. Also, there is the issue of ties.

The distribution of your numbers, specifically the range between your lowest scoring column and your highest scoring column, is analogous to the concept of tint, hue, and shade of a color. For example, blue is still considered blue even if it is dark blue, light blue, French blue, navy blue, or periwinkle. When I discuss the results of *The Power of Understanding People* assessment in seminars, I separate the attendees into four subgroups based on their lowest scoring column. To determine which of the dozen Hollywood styles best describe them, I introduce the second lowest scoring column. It is an easy, efficient and effective way to discuss style during a two to three-hour seminar wherein the goal is to better identify and understand how to deal with others. However, that approach is too simple for extracting Me. There is a difference in a person who scores closer to 12 than to 30 for their low score, for example. Further, a high score above 42 means something entirely different than a high score around 35. The pattern of the results is important.

Ties represent another issue. The mind is not binary. We can have an equal preference for two or even more styles. Although that alone isn't complicated, the result of these dual style preferences can be. Using myself as an example, my preference for column B and column D are the same. For me, this reflects a slightly different thinking orientation when I am operating in a professional context versus a personal context. It is the old, "I am one way at work and a different way at home." The difference is quite subtle, but meaningful. For me, it is just as important to examine how these two style preferences coexist as it is to understand how each defines me. My struggle with two equal preferences informs me as much as the influence of the two individually. In other words, I am both a product of each of those styles *and* the struggle between the two (more on that later). The bottom line is that the wealth of information that can be gleaned from the results of your assessment is huge. It will be important for you to really evaluate not just the order of your preferences, but the degree to which you prefer each relative to another. To aid in this labyrinth of self-examination, let's discuss the three iconic distribution patterns.

The Dynamic Pattern

The bigger the difference between your lowest scoring column and your highest scoring column, the more dynamic your pattern is. For example, if you score below 18 in one column and above 42 in another column, you have a dynamic pattern since you have a large difference between your lowest score (primary preference) and your highest score (quaternary preference). Using the color analogy, your color is more pure, less affected by hue, tint, and shade. Relative to style preference, this dynamic pattern tends to create pure and consistent behavior. People with a dynamic pattern have more obvious (overt) behavioral cues. This means that they display patterns of behavior that others can more easily identify and predict. Additionally, people with dynamic patterns tend to have more consistent and reliable behavioral cues. Regardless of the context within which you interact with them, they tend to behave in the same way.

Consistency of behavior can be very important in your relationships with others in ways that you may not realize. I maintain that whether they like or dislike you, people prefer to form an opinion on you quickly rather than be unsure of how they feel. We can certainly change our opinions of others over time in long-term relationships; but for most of our relationships, we like to connect (or not) quickly. It is easier for people to determine if they like people when they possess dynamic patterns. Consequently, people with dynamic patterns often have enduring and satisfying personal relationships, since others know what to expect from them behaviorally. They are what they are, so to speak. If you like that style, you like them. If you dislike that style, you often self-select out quickly ... with their full support. The exception to this can be family members and coworkers. In both relationships, you are forced to endure each other even if you would prefer not to. And often, over time, you forge relationships despite style differences – or sometimes, because of them.

As a quick aside here, on a topic that will be discussed more comprehensively later in the book, there is an important lesson about human interaction hidden in that last paragraph. We naturally tend to quickly assess whether we connect with someone or not and then create a cognitive schema for them that is positive, negative, or – for a little while maybe – neutral. It is the whole power of the first impression phenomenon. Of course, we make that "decision" initially based on scant knowledge of the full value of the other person. If, however, that person is a family member or a coworker, we continue to have exposure to them over time. This sustained relationship can eventually change our initial impression. Have you ever noticed that the most unusual people at your party – the ones that don't fit the pattern of your other friends – are usually relatives and coworkers. That's because your relationships with them transcended the ease of interaction of a casual friend and includes other qualities. With the growing tribalism and separatism that seems to have consumed our existence in recent times, I think it is valuable to remember the immense advantages of embracing diversity of thought and style.

Another consideration related to the range of totals in the assessment is the correlation to stress. The broader the distribution of numbers, the greater the potential stress when dealing with others. Individuals with a dynamic pattern have a greater potential stress load depending on with whom they are required to interact. Again, family gatherings aside, this stress is more likely to manifest itself at work, because we largely choose our personal relationships. Since few among us get to choose our coworkers and customers, it is at work that we often deal with people who think very differently from us. When fate is the friend of the dynamic pattern, and we get to interact primarily with people who share our style preferences, there will be very little stress. However, when the dynamic pattern is thrust into recurring interactions with people who think very differently than we do, the stress load can be quite high. If you have a dynamic pattern, you may find that your level of professional stress ebbs and flows in larger quantities than individuals who do not have this range of preference. There is nothing abnormal about that. In fact, being aware of these cycles of stress will help you engage in more effective strategies for managing those episodes of high duress.

As you consider the influence of your style preferences on understanding yourself, pay attention to both the heightened impact of your primary style and the effect of a relatively small orientation to your quaternary style. Both are clues to your own gifts, and possessing a dynamic pattern increases their impact. I think of a dynamic pattern as being like a wine that possesses very pronounced qualities, like a tannic Cabernet Sauvignon, a sweet Riesling, a particularly zesty Sauvignon Blanc, or a very fruity Zinfandel. Each of these wines has a wonderful quality that defines it, while also potentially alienating those drinkers who are averse to that characteristic.

Nuanced Pattern

The nuanced pattern is not the *opposite* of the dynamic pattern; as I am fond of saying, "There is no yin yang in Jung!" When the totals of the four columns are clustered in a tight range – like 27 to 33 from highest to lowest – your preferences become subtler. I think of people possessing this pattern as having a high level of cognitive dexterity as it relates to style. They experience less duress when shifting out of their primary style and can even comfortably employ their quaternary style for short periods of time. It's like a color that is hard to discern or appears to change in different light. I have a pair of slacks that look gray sometimes, other times they look brown and, on a few occasions, even green. The nuanced pattern is like that.

If the individual with a nuanced pattern has effectively developed the ability to shift to the desired style appropriate for the situation, this dexterity can be very useful, particularly at work. As referenced earlier, work is where we are often required to interact with individuals whose styles differ from ours. The nuanced pattern allows for rapid, lower stress adaptation to others. Therefore, it is not unusual for nuanced patterned individuals to be effective in a wide variety of situations and with a broad cross-section of the population.

The challenge for this pattern may occur more in their personal lives. Nuanced patterns don't display a consistent behavioral pattern, nor are their behavioral cues as overt. In short, they can be a tougher read for others. Although this characteristic is often a minor issue in more transactional professional relationships, it can frustrate family, friends, and personal acquaintances. There is also the distinct possibility that the nuanced patterned individual will manifest a different style throughout the week, if not the day. I had one wife tell me about her nuanced patterned husband, "I love morning him, evening him ... not so much." I chuckled. Briefly.

In a wine, a nuanced pattern is like your everyday table wine that goes with a wide variety of foods. It is versatile, comfortable, and easy to drink. Perhaps it is a blend of several different varietals. It may take a while to truly appreciate its complexities, but it is reliable in every situation.

Common Pattern

The third iconic distribution of the column totals is the common pattern. Although that doesn't sound very sexy, the common pattern is so named because it is the most frequently occurring distribution. If your low score is 18–26 and your high score is 34–42, you have a common pattern. This means that your style preferences and accompanying duress with adjusting to others are right smack dab in the middle of the bell curve for all people. If you were a wine, it could be said of you that you have *typicity*. Typicity is the degree to which a wine reflects the varietal characteristics of the grape from which it is made. It's a good thing.

Possessing a common pattern on your style preferences can still give you clues about understanding yourself. Examining your primary, secondary, tertiary, and quaternary style preferences is still very important. Less important is the range when examining a common pattern.

About Ties

One final scenario to explore as it relates to the distribution of your column totals is the phenomenon of ties. When administering the short version of the assessment during my seminars,

I have found roughly 5–7% of attendees report a tie for the lowest scoring column (their primary preference). When completing the longer version in this chapter, that percentage drops to under 3%. It is completely possible, perhaps even likely, that an even longer assessment would virtually eliminate these ties. It is also completely possible that some people have the same level of preference for two (or three or – gasp – *four*) styles. I think the relative rarity of the phenomenon after only a 48 variable comparative analysis (a fancy term for the style assessment you just took) is more noteworthy when understanding ourselves. Even if one of the two styles that tied on the assessment is slightly preferable to you – and you can probably figure this out on your own – the influence of having two different style preferences of equal or near equal appeal is meaningful to extracting Me.

To find an example of this, I don't have to look far. My B column and my D column scores are the same and are my two lowest totals. As I will explain in the following chapter, I have learned a lot about myself related to all three of these data points: my low B score, my low D score, and my tie between these two preferences. Based on my conversations with others who have reported out a tie for their primary preference, this can reflect a certain compartmentalization within your life. The most frequent of those is the work-life/home-life compartments. Some people use one of their style preferences more at work and the other at home. In this case, the person is not executing a radically different approach at work versus home but rather shifting one up and the other down.

I recommend that you return to this chapter after reading through the next four chapters. Sometimes it is difficult to understand a concept until you have been exposed to the whole of it. Besides, the next chapter will generate some tangible elements in your extraction. I know for me it is far easier to add in the details once the broad strokes have been brushed. Ask any winemaker about making wine and they will tell you, "it's 40% lifting crap, 40% cleaning crap, and 20% tasting crap." Or 20% doing shots – depending on the wine maker.

Chapter 6 Experts
It's About the Process for Me

> Only the first bottle is expensive.
>
> *– French wine proverb*

Each of the four columns represents a sensitivity to your world. Knowing your level of sensitivity to these four elements of your surroundings is essential to truly understanding and defining your authentic self. In my previous book, *The Power of Understanding People*, I used the terms Expert (A column), Romantic (B column), Mastermind (C column) and Warrior (D column) to label these interactive styles. For readers of both books, I will continue to use those terms while adding a couple more helpful descriptors.

The easiest way to understand your scores is to think of them as reflecting the level of emphasis you place on certain aspects of situations: process, people, possibilities and pace. The A column represents an emphasis on process, the B column on people, the C column on possibilities, and the D column on pace/point. In the following chapters, we will examine the impact of sensitivities –and lack thereof – relative to each of these focal areas. This chapter will focus on the Expert's sensitivity to process.

The range of possible scores in each individual column is 12–48. Any assessment result with a score below 30 in a column indicates an *above average sensitivity* to the corresponding element of your environment being measured. Because that element is process for the A column, it measures the importance a person places on consistence and accuracy. This manifests itself with things like:

- An attention to detail
- A need for dependable structure and rules
- Consistency in execution of tasks
- Accuracy
- Reliable performance and behavior
- Rigidness ("I'm not stubborn, I'm right")
- Deep knowledge in the areas of specialty
- A desire for security
- Appropriateness of behavior/professionalism
- Thorough explanation of thoughts/instructions
- Suspicious of ideas that have not been tested

MEETING THE EXPERT

If your lowest score (or tied for lowest) is in the A column, you are an Expert. Experts trust those things that they know to be true based on a personal and tangible experience with them. They like to know things, as this knowledge helps to ensure that life's situations will unfold in reliable, consistent ways. Experts thrive in secure environments where there is ample structure, policy, and guidance. It is important to Experts that they not make mistakes, yet another reason they seek out knowledge and rules. For all these reasons, the process becomes the focal point for the Experts as they seek to eliminate the possibility of mistake and chaos. They are generally risk averse. Experts' most pressing intrinsic need is security. They thrive when they feel that their environment is well established and safe.

Your preferred style influences the way you execute your core ideology. If you think of life vision as a journey to a desired future state and core ideology as the vehicle within which you will travel, then your style is how you look as you travel along. And although your interactive style alone does not define you, it does inform you. It is what others notice first about you. It is critical to how you communicate and how you like to be rewarded. It is also the lens through which you view the world. Therefore, understanding how your style shapes both who you are and how others see you is essential to extracting Me. The Expert is shaped by risk aversion, the pursuit of perfection, and reliability.

The pursuit and possession of knowledge that is at the root of the Expert style can often result in some very deep analysis of information. Consequently, Experts often display few non-verbal cues. They possess the classic poker face. In fact, when I teach communication, client service, and consultative-selling-skills classes, I tell my attendees that the behavioral cue of the Expert is the lack of behavioral cues. The difference between sorrow and joy on the face of an Expert can be virtually indistinguishable.

THE BEHAVIORAL CUES (OR LACK THEREOF) OF EXPERTS

I remember speaking to a group of chemical engineers in Lake Jackson, Texas about 15 years ago. There were 35 attendees, and the human resources department had hired me because the team was experiencing challenges communicating with one another. I arrived at the facility one hour before my scheduled 9:00 a.m. class. The congenial receptionist directed me to the training room. It was this room that provided me with the first incontrovertible evidence that this was a very Expert culture at the facility. The training room was decorated in early ... penitentiary. Everything was white on white, interrupted only by the occasional piece of masking tape with a word neatly written by Sharpie: "LCD Projector," "Laptop," etc. I quickly set up my audio/visual equipment and prepared for my three-hour course on communication.

At 8:57 a.m., all 35 participants filed into the training room in silence, signed a company attendance sheet, took their seats, and opened their notebooks. Three minutes later, I began. Remember: my motto is "laugh and learn." I have been a professional speaker for over 20 years and before devoting all my efforts to speaking, I worked in jobs that required me to speak publicly a good deal of the time. Essentially, I have been compensated wholly or in part for public speaking since I was 16 years old. It is a skill that I have honed, and using humor is a large part of that. I share this simply to reinforce that *I know where the funny is*. I also know that even the best humor can miss its mark occasionally.

So when I offered my first funny anecdote to the 35 chemical engineers and they didn't laugh, it wasn't the lack of a guffaw that knocked me off balance. It was the fact that they took notes. They *wrote the funny*. Who does that? Well, apparently Experts who score with dynamic patterns do. I would later discover that almost all of the attendees scored below 18 in the A column. Unfortunately, I wasn't practicing metacognition. Rather than realizing the style of my audience and adjusting my expectations of their response, I doggedly pursued my own intrinsic needs.

You know the story of the mechanic whose own car doesn't run? Or the doctor who is in poor health? How about the one where the educator on metacognition fails to practice metacognition? That was me. I got stuck inside my own head and my Me desires appreciation. I derive that appreciation on stage by the audience's reaction. So, the lack of laughter was a negative motivator that inspired me to throw more effort into my delivery. Making matters worse for me was my other intrinsic need – winning. I wanted to be liked and win, and I decided upping the energy would achieve *my* needs. After an hour, I was essentially Richard Simmons on methamphetamines – racing around the room, spinning, sweating, and trying to *will* the room to a reaction. At about the two-hour mark, I had an out-of-body experience. I was mentally hovering over myself in that classroom watching me flail about in a futile effort to generate some response from my deeply analytical attendees. Finally, after three hours, I retired to the door of the training room and prepared for the mercy killing at the end of the class.

To my surprise, all 35 attendees lined up in front of me like I was the bride at a wedding reception. One by one they came up to me, shook my hand and said, "that was the best training class we have ever had here." They then proceeded to walk out of the room in complete silence with no expression on their face. I still get emails from the human resources people at that company that say, "Those guys still talk about you." I respond, "And I still talk about *them*."

AN EXPERT IS A WINE'S ACIDITY

The wine world comparison of the Expert style could be the complicated concepts of wine and food pairings. Even the most adept sommelier can get uneasy when asked to pair elaborate meals with the "perfect" wine. Imagine how challenging that is? When you consider all the ingredients, flavors, and consistency of food and the complexities and sheer number of wines in the world and to come up with an exceptional match off the top of your head! I get a panic attack just thinking about it. Acidity, one of the four traits of wine, is my go-to consideration when selecting a wine to pair with food. Acidity makes the mouth salivate, so it is an insurance policy for overcooked poultry. Acidity cuts through fatty and fried food. For my money, with a few exceptions, you rarely go wrong pairing food with Champagne or Pinot Noir. In that way, the Expert style is to the mind as acidity is to the wine. They both provide safety and reliability even in the most complicated of circumstances.

As an educator, I strive to provide learning experiences that are fun *and* informative. I refer to my style as *enter-"train"- ment*. I also love to integrate my love for wine with my passion for understanding our own minds. One of my most popular programs is *What Is Your Wine Personality?* When I select a wine that reflects the Expert style, the two characteristics that are most important are acidity and nuance. To me, that captures the way an expert mind works: acidity because it allows the wine to be versatile as a food pairing (a safe choice), and nuance because it reflects the technical prowess of the winemaker.

Imagine you had an inherent need to reduce risk. How could you best satisfy this need? Well, learning everything you could possibly know about a subject would be a solid strategy. Experts use knowledge to mitigate risk.

But what about those of us who score above 30 in the A column? For example, my score on this assessment is 37. It is my tertiary (third) preference among the four styles. I was quite surprised by this, given my professional choices (to start my own business), frequent moves all around the country (I have lived more than a decade in each of Illinois, Florida, and Colorado, and am now living in Washington), and general optimism when it comes to assuming risk.

Don't get me wrong; a 37 score would indicate that the Expert style and the need for processes are not very high for me. It is just a higher preference than I expected. But, my lovely bride would be quick to point out the many routines I employ when traveling and even at home that indicate that I *do* have some need for consistency and structure. I enjoy traveling but after too long on the road I long for a week or two of the same bed, same time zone, and the comfort of a stable schedule.

More importantly to you, a score higher than 30 in the A column will likely mean that your core ideology will not revolve around processes. Whatever approach you utilize toward fulfilling your calling will *not* include a detailed and structured approach. That's not to say that you can't develop a strength for organization and compliance; it's just that it would be unusual for you to find your true joy in these elements of your world. You may find that time spent with processes causes you stress or, at the very least, drains you of energy. This does not mean you should avoid processes altogether. Life requires all of us to work outside our essence from time to time. Knowing why certain tasks, situations, and even people can require more effort – to be accompanied by greater psychic cost – is very useful to understanding ourselves.

As you examine your assessment utilizing the context of all four column scores, you will have greater nuance and perspective. For now, consider what your score in column A may tell you about yourself. If your score is below 30, how does your preference for the Expert style inform the way you behave, think, and interact with others? Remember, as the score gets lower, the preference and influence increases. If you have a score below 20, the Expert style has a large impact on you. Conversely, if you score is above 30, how does that help to define you? And if that score is above 40, the Expert influence becomes notable in its lack of impact. Use the extracting Me Worksheet to write your thoughts on how the Expert style contributes to Me.

Our goal is to integrate our knowledge of our relative style preferences into our core ideology to obtain a deeper and broader definition of Me. So far, we have only examined one of the four styles. Let's turn our attention to the B column and see the influence of people on our essence.

Chapter 7 Romantics

It's About the People for Me

> Drink freely the wine life offers you and
> don't worry how much you spill.
>
> – *Marty Rubin*

If your lowest score falls in the B column, then you have developed a more heightened sensitivity to emotions. Somehow, probably during your teen years, you became more aware of the feeling content within your environment. You experience emotion more deeply than many other people and this informs how you construct your delusion and how you communicate with others. I can relate, as my score in the B Column is a 20, tied for my lowest score.

I refer to the low B's as the Romantics. Your emotional sensitivity makes you more empathetic and even sympathetic to others' perspectives. Even if your score in this column is not your lowest score, a total below 30 indicates a sensitivity to feelings. Here are some common attributes associated with Romantics:

- Tactful and diplomatic communicator
- Willing mediator
- Prefers to minimize or avoid conflict
- Aware of the impact of actions on emotions of others
- Good at delivering both good and bad news
- Self-sacrificing, altruistic
- A good team player
- Susceptible to emotional manipulation from others (e.g., guilt)
- Influenced by the prevailing emotion(s) in their environment
- A good counselor
- Quick to praise others

MEETING THE ROMANTIC

The key to understanding your core ideology as a Romantic is that you will always be aware and influenced by the feelings of those around you and important to you. There is no dishonor in that, for sure. Romantics make the world a more thoughtful and caring place. It is a gift to be this intuitive on the nature of emotions. But, like all gifts, that sensitivity to feelings can also be a burden. For example, when Romantics sacrifices their own needs to ensure that those around them have their needs met first, it can have a very positive affect on team morale and function. But, since Romantics rarely asks for anything in return – although they would love to be appreciated for that sacrifice – there are times that they may feel that others take them for granted or take advantage of them. It is important for Romantics to learn how to reconcile their inherent willingness to help others with the possibility that others won't always recognize or reward their efforts.

If you are a Romantic, it is also essential to understand that feeling appreciated is your most important intrinsic need. I have met several Romantics who have told me that they do not care if others appreciate them. My reaction is, "Bullshit." It would take very, very, *very* self-actualized Romantics to sacrifice their own needs without *any* need to be appreciated, even on a small scale, for that behavior. And it is entirely okay to have that need. All people need some level of security, appreciation, excitement, and independence to feel fulfilled. For Romantics, the appreciation reward just runs a little higher, just as security is a little more important to Experts.

Another important consideration is that emotions emanate from people. While Experts are keenly aware of how processes work, Romantics focus on the human element. It would be hard for me to imagine a Romantic having a core ideology that excludes some relationship with people. If you scored under 30 in the B column, you are likely going to integrate some component of relationships into your true self.

PUTTING OTHERS' HAPPINESS BEFORE YOUR OWN

Since I am a Romantic, I of course have a personal story that relates. In fact, I have so many that I find myself trying to sort out just one to share as I write this chapter. I settled on this one because it is both simple and telling. My lovely bride and I have been married for 32 years as I write this book. I knew we were destined to be together when my beloved New York Mets won their second World Series the same year we were wed. (I have not held her responsible for the fact that, as of this writing, they have not won another, but I digress.) When you pass a certain anniversary "mile marker," you are granted automatic membership in the marriage-advice club. I am often asked what the secret to a long and happy relationship is. My answer is distinctly Romantic:

"Marry someone whose happiness is more important to you than your own, and who feels the same about you."

I do find it somewhat defeating that most people just respond to this with a "hmm" and change the subject. It is brilliant in its simplicity, at least to my way of thinking. I realize that there is nothing pragmatic, aspirational, or even remotely profound about the statement. But, it has worked for my lovely bride and me for all these years. I am also aware that I devoted an entire chapter to internal locus of control and how your happiness is your own responsibility. (You know, the life-is-like-stew talk.) But, love is weird. Love is always the exception. So, in my opinion, if you find someone who is devoted to your happiness and to whose happiness *you* are devoted, marry that person. Oh, and my lovely bride is a Romantic, too. So, this advice quite likely only works if you are a Romantic who fell in love with a Romantic. That's why I didn't write a book about marriage. I may have just gotten lucky.

REFRAMING CHILDHOOD TRIALS

This strikes me as a good time to discuss another important component of extracting Me. Since a large part of who we are is developed in those years between birth and around 22 years of age, we should consider how both the positive and negative aspects of our youth may have contributed to our current state. We learn to think and believe in certain ways in response to our early life experiences. Although they may have been quite useful to us at, say, 14 years of age, these same ways of thinking might be self-limiting at age 34. Again, that is the value of metacognition.

But, there is more to understanding ourselves than just taking inventory on how we think. Sometimes we need to redefine our own history. Sometimes, challenging or even tragic life events that occurred when we were young can provide the foundation for greater strength as we age. This is why it's so important to redefine adversity into a mechanism for strength.

I am convinced that my pronounced emotional sensitivity has its origins in just such adversity. Growing up in a household that concealed the secret of addiction and the related toxic elements, I honed my awareness of others' states of mind. My mother's relationship with alcohol struck me as a severe allergy; it only took a few drinks for her demeanor to dramatically change. There was no question in my mind that adding alcohol to her brain chemistry created a volatile reaction. Her behavior became erratic, then contentious and, eventually, violent with the transition from tranquility to volatility occurring with dizzying speed. I learned to recognize each behavioral cue early and do my best to delay the inevitable spot within her toxic targeting. Eventually, I was able to glean her psychological status within a few seconds of walking into the house. My mother – indirectly and in a manner that she would have not preferred, to be sure – provided me with a doctoral level ability of deciphering another's emotional state.

The few who know the details of my youth are quick to say supportive things. "You are so fortunate to have not been affected by that environment," they will say. But that's not true. I was. I am quite convinced that my deep sensitivity to the emotional elements around me are the direct result of my experiences growing up. As an adult, I use this sensitivity to counsel others; to try to spread joy; to be a better husband, father, and person. Although my youth may have seemed difficult, I feel strongly that those trials contributed significantly to my best attributes.

My point for you is, don't discount the *v*alue of your tribulations. We are quick to draw a direct line between adversity and vulnerability, but there also close relationship between our pain and our gifts. By reframing our most difficult experiences from painful memories to valuable moments of growth, we not only free ourselves from the ghosts of our past – we provide a reason to celebrate our strengths. It is my belief that all people share this part of humanity and certainly none more than Romantics.

A ROMANTIC IS A WINE'S SWEETNESS

If Experts are analogous to acidity in wine, then Romantics would be the sweetness. Sugar is essential to the fermentation process, for without it there would be no wine. In fact, the brix – the measurement of sugar in the grape – is one of the most essential measurements for determining when to harvest. Sugar literally *starts* the winemaking process. It is consumed by yeast during fermentation and the result is the alcohol content of the wine. And the alcohol content – well, let's just say that's when the party starts! I mean, every wine drinker I know would be telling a white lie if they didn't admit that part of the attraction of the beverage was the influence of the alcohol. The same can be said about Romantics. If you want to have a great party, invite plenty of Romantics. Just as the sugar in a grape, Romantics will kick things off and make sure that everyone has a good time.

When selecting a wine that reflects the Romantic style in my tasting seminars, I focus on two iconic characteristics: the influence of sugar and the approachability of the wine. Romantics are easy to be around and integral to good times. Living in Walla Walla, Washington, where the summer days are long, sunny, and hot, and the season lasts for half the year, we love our Rosés.

Please indulge me while I engage in a personal crusade on behalf of the value of drinking Rosé. Many of us started our personal wine journeys with the infamous White Zinfandel – the gateway drug to a lifetime of wine-fueled good times. White Zinfandel is very sweet and lacks complexity. Think of it as that super nice friend that is a pleasure to be around – but whose conversation is always very superficial. They don't challenge you and, after a short amount of time, may be kind of boring. That is *not* representative of Rosé, nor is it reflective of the Romantic style. Rosé wines run the gamut from dry to sweet, simple to complex. They are not even the same color. Some Rosé wines are nearly white, others have an orange hue, and many fall in all shades of pink.

There are few things so fun, so enchanting, and so relaxing as enjoying a well made Rosé while sitting outside on a beautiful day with friends while people watching. Rosé is laughter's elixir. So, insofar as Rosé is an essential element of celebration of friends, fun, and frolic, it is perfect as a reflection of the Romantic style.

As you think about yourself relative to your score in the B column, you are considering the degree to which you can quickly and accurately gauge the emotional status of those around you. If your score is below 18, you have an incredible capacity for this. In fact, this ability may very well be the cornerstone of your core ideology. Go back and read the explanation of "dynamic patterns" in Chapter 5, which introduces style. Keep in mind, if your score is below 18, that sensitivity to emotion may have some challenges, too. Being extremely sensitive to emotion can make you even more vulnerable to manipulation, feelings of guilt, or being overwhelmed by prevailing emotions in your environment. If your score is below 30, emotional sensitivity has at least some impact on how you navigate your world. If your score is above 30, others' feelings have a lesser impact on you. That can be an important realization as you construct your core ideology, too. There are many situations that require the ability to ignore how others will feel about something to accomplish what is necessary.

Spend a little time reflecting on what your Romantic column score might mean relative to your core ideology and document these thoughts on the Extracting Me Worksheet.

Chapter 8 Masterminds

It's About the Possibilities for Me

WINE! Because these problems aren't
going to forget themselves!

– Tanya Masse

If your lowest score is in column C, you are a Mastermind –
and your greatest sensitivity is to concepts. Masterminds view
yesterday as boring, today as mildly amusing, but tomorrow ...
well, tomorrow is *full* of possibilities. I have found Masterminds to display what the French call *je ne sais quoi* – a term
that refers to a quality that is hard to describe or even pinpoint,
but that makes them special or interesting.

The Mastermind column is my highest scoring column at
43. So, apparently, I do *not* have that *je ne sais quoi*. My lovely bride, on the other hand, does. Her score in the C column
is her second-lowest score. So, she has long been my research
subject for the influence that the Mastermind style has on

a person's behavior. Here are some attributes that can be common to Masterminds:

- Comfortable in loosely defined situations
- Embraces risk
- More comfortable with trial and error
- Enjoys doing new things and having unusual experiences
- May appear scattered or unfocused
- Bores easily with routines
- Capable of juggling several tasks simultaneously
- Easily distracted by events or people that they view as more interesting than their current activity
- Generally optimistic that things will turn out well
- Enjoys brainstorming ideas

MEETING THE MASTERMIND

In true Mastermind style, let me digress for a moment and criticize one of the most iconic and useful psychological devices. I have two pet peeves when it comes to the myriad of style-assessment tools that exist for helping us better understand how we think. One is that they often report out in a strict binary fashion. By this, I mean they tell you that your results are either this or that. I understand that this is frequently just a shortcut employed by the evaluator to make it simple for the recipient to understand their results. However, it does remove some very important details. Masterminds will surely nod in agreement that *any* evaluative device that works on a black-and-white format is inherently limiting. Masterminds exist in a world of gray. Theirs is not a toggle switch world, but a three-dimensional sliding attenuator. For example, if you take a Myers-Briggs Type Indicator (MBTI), you will be told you are an ENTJ (Extroversion, Intuition, Thinking, Judgment) or an ISFP (Introversion, Sensory, Feeling, Perception) or one of the other 16 total combinations. But there is a big difference in two ENTJs, for example, when you explore the range of their preferences. That is why I referenced the differences between a dynamic pattern, common pattern, and nuanced pattern in Chapter 5. All styles, but none more than the Mastermind, recognize that two people with the same labeled results can still be quite different.

My second irritant is the insistence of many assessment tools to place human behavior into quadrants. Quadrants suggest opposites and make it difficult for a person to be at or near in preference for the two opposing quadrants. But human behavior doesn't work that way. Again, Masterminds particularly would take umbrage to being placed neatly into a quadrant. One of the inspirations for my own approach to understanding interactive style was rooted in my MBTI results. I scored as an INFJ. It fits loosely, but so does the INTJ. I realized that my results in the F (Feeler) and T (Thinker) were close to the same. So, while I reported as a Feeler, I was almost just as influenced by my Thinker. Further, the internal conflict that I experience – and which would be critical to my own extraction of Me – was much more the result of that Feeler/Thinker conflict than it was the influence of the N (Intuitive). Practitioners of the MBTI understand this, but it is very difficult to share all these subtleties in a classroom setting to individuals who just want to know how they can effectively utilize the information. So, it is a pet peeve.

Beyond the free plug for the work of Isabel Myers and Katharine Briggs, there is a point to my venting. More than any other style, the Mastermind values individuality. Taking an interactive style assessment, no matter how well researched and validated, still feels too much like a one-size-fits-all experience to Masterminds. Masterminds live to venture outside of the containments that life attempts to force upon them. In fact, rules, policies, procedures, regulations – these are all "food for thought" for Masterminds. "Thanks for the input," a Mastermind might say as they summarily dismiss it.

BREAKING THE RULE IN ORDER TO FOLLOW THE RULE

Because my own score in the C column is high, I am not much of a rule breaker myself (my reckless youth aside.) But with the help of a Mastermind fellow traveler, I did just that. This story has its origins in my own inner style conflict and the odd duality of my profession. I do both business development and service delivery for my company. In most organizations, there exists a (usually) healthy conflict between those who do the selling and those doing the service. It is not unusual for the service people to feel that the sales people have overpromised. Likewise, it is not unusual for the sales people to accuse the service folks of whining.

So, there are times when, in my role as business development person, I commit to some pretty gnarly travel logistics in order to close a deal on a speaking engagement. I always check to make sure that it is feasible on paper; but I don't always consider what it will be like when I actually have to *do* it. That was the case when I accepted speaking engagements in San Francisco, Paris, and Las Vegas in the same week. It is *possible*. The flights worked. It can be done. But the reality from a service delivery perspective was brutal. Faced with the reality of the travel, I was quite aggravated with the person who had arranged it. Had I been able to, I would have fired me. That's how I felt when I was sitting in the San Francisco airport, staring at the upgrade list, using every bit of my "thoughts and prayers" to get the last upgrade to business class.

I have flown nearly two million miles on United Airlines. They carry me on board while feeding me grapes ... for domestic flights. It's nice. But, there is much less special treatment for international flights. Forget first class; that is limited to the likes of the Kardashians. I just wanted to escape coach and get into business class. On this flight, the seats were like a domestic flight's first class. Not incredibly comfortable, but compared to coach, they were like love seats. Plus, you got the occasional glass of wine and recognizable food. If you have flown coach class on an international flight that will last approximately

12 hours you know that there is no relaxing allowed. By the time you reach your destination, coach class appears to have been the site of a violent social uprising barely suppressed by the flight crew. There are newspapers, trash, blankets, food products, magazines, footwear, and even livestock strewn wil-ly-nilly around the cabin. No, I knew I couldn't relax in coach. I had to have a business class upgrade.

For better or worse, I am not sure which, United provides you with a ton of metrics and data to analyze relative to your upgrade status. For instance, I knew how many business class seats were available on this plane – 24. I also knew how many business class tickets were purchased – also 24 (damn!). Final-ly, I knew that 23 people had checked in for those 24 seats. So, that means that one passenger had bought a business class seat but had not yet checked in for their flight from San Francisco to Paris as we approached one hour before takeoff. Oh, and guess who was at the very *top* of the upgrade list for any avail-able business class seats. Um hmm. Dave Mitchell – or as I am known on an upgrade list, D/MIT (which I also feel could be my rapper name). Anyway …

I consider myself a kind person. I am a Romantic, after all. But on this occasion, I was rooting for a "minor" in-cident involving the last, unchecked-in business class pas-senger. You know, like a last-minute change in travel plans or a fender bender on the way to the airport. Or maybe he or she won the lottery yesterday and quit their job and no longer needed to go to Paris. Or they were arrested. Any-thing! The gate agent increased both my excitement and my anxiety by announcing, "Passenger Mitchell, please remain in the boarding area for a possible upgrade." The upside of that was that I still had a chance. The downside is that I got to watch 500 passengers, each with two pieces of luggage, board before me. If I didn't get the upgrade now, I would need to place my bag in an overhead bin roughly a quarter mile behind my seat. The only thing worse than flying in coach is trying to move against the current to get your bag once you land.

Then it happened. The gate agent called me to the desk. "We've upgraded you to business class, Mr. Mitchell."

I am pretty sure that elevated this *particular* day to my fourth best ever after only my wedding and the birth of my two children. The bounce in my step as I bopped down the jetway to my plane belied my level of happiness and more than a little cockiness. I even scored an aisle seat. Nothing could interrupt my euphoria. Well ... not until I sat down in my seat and it reclined on its own.

Anyone who travels much knows there are a few absolute truths about air travel. For instance, on each flight there will be one person in your row who absolutely must visit the washroom repeatedly; your first choice for a snack will be sold out before the flight attendants reach your seat; a child seated behind inexplicably finds joy in the act of kicking the seat in front of them ... and during takeoff and landing, you must stow your tray table, fasten your seatbelt and place your seat back in its full upright position. It is, so we are told, an FAA regulation. Despite a lifelong commitment to core exercise, I could not keep my seat back from creeping into recline. The dutiful flight attendant, likely an Expert, approached me as we neared our departure time.

"Excuse me, sir, but I will need you to bring your seat into the upright position for takeoff," she offered with a smile.

"I completely understand, and I am certainly not being a malcontent," I responded in my best Romantic. "I am a lifetime million-mile flyer and Premier Platinum United flyer," I added that strategically in hopes that my status might somehow exempt me from our nation's laws. "The problem is the seat won't stay in the upright position," and with that I demonstrated my plight by showing the flight attendant my hands while the seat slowly reclined. I guess I am a tertiary Expert, huh?

"Oh, that's unfortunate. Because if your seat isn't fully functional, for your safety and the safety of those around you, we will need to reseat you."

"*Oh hell no!*" Okay, I didn't actually say that, but Lord knows I thought it. The flight attendant walked away to attend to some other compliance concern of grave FAA consequences and I went full MacGyver on the seat. I dove into my briefcase for resources. I was bound and determined to repair the broken seat using my eyeglass screwdriver, a flash drive, and four Tic Tacs. I was in a full state of panic as I imagined the next 12 hours trapped, unrelaxed, in coach. Just then, the passenger next to me violated all the rules of business class travel and talked to me.

"I couldn't help but overhear your situation. I have an idea."

"You have an idea for my situation?" Fortunately, my incredulous tone did not dissuade my row mate from pressing forward.

"Yes, if you are interested," he persisted. In retrospect, I realize that he surveyed the tools I had assembled and was confident that I would indeed be open to suggestions.

"Absolutely!"

"Cool. So, I think that takeoff and landing are the busiest times for the flight attendants. They have to check for seatbelts being fastened, bags being properly stowed, tray tables put away and, of course, the seat backs being upright. So I'm pretty sure they use some hacks to do that quickly."

"Hacks?" I repeated.

He continued, "You know, shortcuts. For seat backs, I think they look at the relationship between the seats in the row. If they are aligned, then they assume both are upright. If they aren't, they know someone needs to bring their seat to the upright position. Since you can't keep your seat from reclining, maybe I could recline mine. That way they would be aligned, and she may think they are both upright. What do you think?"

The sheer genius of his suggestion left me in awe. "I think that is an excellent idea." I quickly replaced my eyeglass screwdriver, mints, and flash drive in my brief case while he discreetly reclined his seat. Soon, the flight attendant came through the cabin scanning each row for unbuckled seat belts, stray bags, noncompliant tray tables and the rogue seat back. She sailed right past us and shortly thereafter, we took off and I "high fived" my new best friend.

"You don't know how much I needed this seat. Thank you so much. You, sir, are a life saver." My unbridled joy seemed about twice again too much for the situation, but I was doubly excited. "What's especially cool about this is that not only did you save my business class seat; you also gave me a great story for my seminars in the future." I went on to explain that I spoke professionally on the topic of applied cognitive psychology and described how I wrote about people's different styles in *The Power of Understanding People*.

I decided to indulge in a bit of instruction. "The flight attendant, who was dutifully fulfilling her obligations to attend to passenger security by consistently applying FAA regulations, is most likely an Expert. Experts like structure and are committed to compliance and security. You, on the other hand, display a willingness to take chances, circumvent the rules, and find an alternative to achieve the desired result. So, you are probably a Mastermind. I have to ask, what do *you* do for a living?"

"I'm a pilot."

I remember the silence that followed was a bit uncomfortable.

Anyway, a couple of takeaways here: if you are a Mastermind or have scored below 30 in the C column even if another column was lower, this ability – even desire – to work outside the structured environment likely plays a role in understanding yourself. Many entrepreneurs have a low C column score. They are comfortable with a somewhat vague vision of tomorrow providing them guidance for today's actions. Their willingness, even eagerness, to experiment and learn from mistakes armors them against the risk involved.

Takeaway two: when flying, it is very likely that the flight attendants care deeply about your safety even though, meanwhile, they aren't even wearing seatbelts up in the cockpit.

A MASTERMIND IS A WINE'S FRUIT

Revisiting the wine-industry metaphor, if Experts are like acidity and Romantics are like sugar, then the Masterminds are the fruit. When people find out that I am an advanced sommelier, they often ask what my favorite wine is. That is an impossible question to answer. First, there are over 10,000 varieties of grape, so if a person decided to experience every one of them by trying a different wine made from each varietal every day, it would take them 28 years – and probably three livers – to experience them all. That doesn't even take into account the countless number of blends, wines that use more than one variety of grape, that exist. There are likely millions of individual types of wines produced by these 10,000 unique varietals. You can spend your entire life drinking a different type of wine each day and never experience them all. *That* is so Mastermind-like. Imagine the possibilities!

I would go one step further. Not only are the Masterminds like the uniqueness of the grapes, but they also reflect the intrigue of unknown regions. Cabernet Sauvignon is most associated with Napa in California and Bordeaux in France, but those are far from the only two wine regions that make amazing Cabernet Sauvignon. The Mastermind style is analogous to finding one of the most common and popular grapes grown in a fascinating, exotic location or with a fabulous story to accompany it. One such story is that of the Super Tuscan wines of Italy and it is distinctly Mastermind.

Tuscany experienced incredible political and social changes in the 1950s and 1960s. One of these changes was the elimination of *mezzadria* – a system for farming that outlined the financial arrangement between landowners and the farmers who used the land. Essentially, the changes resulted in the tenant farmers leaving and landowners trying to figure out what to do with this resource that they owned but had no experience with. Many landowners decided to grow grapes and make wines, but few knew what they were doing.

Through trial and error, some maverick thinkers in the wine industry hit on the idea of using grapes that were not *technically* legal to create a new Tuscan wine that would reinvigorate the region. One of the grapes they used was Cabernet Sauvignon. To produce a new wine, the novice winemakers blended the indigenous Sangiovese grape with a grape from

Bordeaux, Cabernet Sauvignon. Today, Super Tuscan wines are among the world's most prestigious. Back in the 1970s, when a few inspired Masterminds came up with the idea of blending unsanctioned grapes with the indigenous grapes of Tuscany, the wine was in blatant violation of the established norms. In that way, I think the Super Tuscan wines are an especially appropriate metaphor for the Mastermind style.

Now it is time to reflect again. As was the case for the Expert and Romantic styles, consider what insights you can glean from your score in the Mastermind column. What does it say about your risk tolerance? Do you thrive in unstructured environments or are you more comfortable having a well-defined system surrounding you? Do you like to know what to expect each day or do you crave the excitement of a situation in flux?

Keep in mind that high scores are helpful to understanding yourself, too. My score of 43 in this column surprised me, and I am certain this reflects a change in my life over the past 20 or maybe even 10 years. That is a valuable insight as I work to maintain my alignment. Perhaps it is reflective of me approaching retirement, although I have no desire to do so. Maybe it represents the joy I have discovered by working on our land. For some reason, I have dropped my need for excitement and risk while elevating my desire for consistency and structure.

Sounds like I have some changes to make in my core ideology. Off I go to the Extracting Me Worksheet.

Chapter 9 Warriors

It's About the Pace and the Point for Me

> Beer is made by men, wine by God.
>
> – *Martin Luther*

There is something just a little mischievous about the placement of the D Column. The D column measures your logical sensitivity. Logic relates to efficiency. If your lowest score is in the D column—or if you score below 30—you have a clear desire to *get to the result*. "Done" is the most desired word in your vocabulary. So, the fact that I made you wait until I had already explained the other three columns is a bit malicious. Of course, it is just as likely that you skipped the previous three chapters and came directly here after you saw your results. That wouldn't surprise me in the least.

I refer to the low D's as the Warriors. A Warrior's mind operates with a time/value ratio evaluator that is constantly utilized to determine one's approach to life events. It is important for the Warrior to minimize time and maximize value. As a result, they put pressure on people and situations to get to the point as quickly as possible. Investing less time takes pressure off the value. Maximizing the value justifies the expenditure of more time. Here are some common attributes associated with Warriors:

- Direct, to-the-point communicator
- Comfortable with conflict
- Competitive
- Results-oriented
- Rules are good for others, but not always necessary for them
- Do not suffer fools gladly
- Intense
- Actions and conversations have purpose
- Fair, but not necessarily equal
- Strategic
- Reward by providing independence

MEETING THE WARRIOR

If your score is below 30 in the Warrior column, and particularly if your D column is the lowest scoring column, this style informs your perspective. My score is 20 and it is tied for my lowest score. We Warriors are often a bit unsettled by processes that remain in progress for extended periods of time. We push toward closure. The simple joy of checking off an item on our to-do list – and rest assured that *all* Warriors have some form of a to-do list – is one of life's great pleasures.

I have found that the real value of cognitive assessments is not that they reinforce what you already know about yourself, but rather when they uncover an explanation for something that you were less familiar with. For example, I have never been surprised when a psychological test tells me that

I am emotionally sensitive. But, so many times, I have wondered about another part of me that isn't explained to my satisfaction. As I mentioned before, I love the MBTI, but my score of INFJ (Introversion, Intuition, Feeling, Judgment) never seemed to fit snugly. That was part of why I developed my own approach.

Discovering that I prefer logic just as much as emotion was a revelation. It helped explain my compulsion for productivity, the frustration I would experience with situations that were not progressing, and my desire to engage in conflict resolution (effective or not) rather than just ignore it. My own internal conflict can, in large part, be explained by the tug of emotion against logic.

Although it is natural to concentrate on big, life-altering insights when engaged in metacognition, sometimes it is fun to identify the root cause of your behavior in the most mundane of circumstances. Recently, Lori and I were with some friends at a local winery that was featuring karaoke. We were enjoying the enthusiasm, and occasional talent, of our comrades displaying their fondness for all kinds of genres. However, I noted a troubling lack of some real headbangers. Most of the song choices were love ballads or country pop songs. I felt like a good old classic rocker, say "You Shook Me All Night Long" by AC/DC, would inject some more energy into the room. The Romantic (and my stage performer) inside me was itching to grab the microphone. But, the Warrior inside me reminded me that my skills as a singer had been well established in college – a story I will share later. Let's just say, if I were to launch a music career, my band should be named Tone Deaf. Doing something poorly is particularly unattractive to Warriors. Despite the best efforts of my inner Romantic, my Warrior style kept me on the sidelines.

For Warriors, nothing is as important as the scoreboard. In that regard, sports become a wonderful reflection of the Warrior mind. There is a winner and a loser, and both are measured by specific metrics that will be publicly displayed until the game is over. That is just beautiful to Warriors. It is not how well a team plays (Experts), not how creative the game plan (Masterminds), or the sportsmanship (Romantics) that determine success. One does not win championships based on those considerations. It is the scoreboard, baby. To the victors go the spoils.

Warriors view life through the lens of efficiency. They want to know what the the most direct path to the desired result is. That is the path they wish to remain on and move quickly along. Anything that slows them or forces them off that path becomes irritating. They aren't ones for small talk, unnecessary meetings, phone calls, silly paperwork, or even unnecessary management. Their intrinsic need is independence. As leaders, they will often tell you that, "No news is good news," as it relates to receiving feedback from them. And if you lead a Warrior, frequently managing their contributions would be the quickest way to ensure they quit. "Do you like my work? Yes? Then leave me alone."

NO ROOM FOR INTERESTING DETAILS

While evaluating my own life "inputs," it should not have been a surprise that the Warrior style would be so dominate in my cognition. My father was clearly a Warrior, a fact that was confirmed when he completed the assessment several years ago. Given my mother's challenges, he was left to be my primary caregiver. That was a role he was distinctly unqualified for. Apparently, fighting in World War II, surviving the Great Depression, and succeeding against all odds to create a successful small business did not provide the appropriate experience for being a nurturing parent. I admired my father. He had many fantastic qualities. Warmth was not among them.

I have one specific memory of my father's, ahem, *counseling* skills. I was 17 years old. By that time, I had been working summers and vacations for nearly five years at my father's appliance store. My dad recognized quickly that keeping me busy and off the streets was a good strategy for my positive development. Anyway, I was out on a service call one afternoon to fix a customer's washing machine. Some members of the high school yearbook staff came into the store to get a picture of me for a story they were doing on how the senior class spent summer vacation. Dad directed them to the customer's home (it's a small-town thing). So, much to my surprise, two of the prettiest girls in the senior class – in which there were only about 90 kids total – showed up to take my picture.

It makes me smile to remember it now, but at the time I was so self-conscious. At 17, the presence of pretty girls made me incredibly nervous. Add to that, I was dirty, unkempt, and completely unprepared for this unannounced visit. Making it all the worse was the utilitarian way the two classmates handled the task. They briefly announced the purpose of their visit, snapped two photos, and left with no more than three sentences of interaction. It's not like they didn't know me. In the 11 preceding years of school, only a handful of classmates had moved into or out of town. So, these two girls had shared many classes and school events with me over the years. The manner in which they showed up, executed their chore, and exited all in the span of five minutes with nary a pleasantry was bruising to a teenage boy's ego.

After completing the service call, I returned to the store. It was clear, even to my emotionally restricted father, that I was bummed.

"What happened to you?" He attempted to engage in some form of venting process.

Reluctantly, I shared. "Well, these two girls from my class came over while I was doing the service call and took my picture for a yearbook story. They are very popular. They barely even talked to me."

"Cheer up, it gets worse." And with that, Dad returned to the task at hand. I remember thinking, *"Really! 'Cheer up, it gets worse?' That has got to be the worst motivational speech I have ever heard in my life."*

Years later, as Dad softened with age and the awareness of his own mortality, his Warrior side softened. I reminded him of that conversation. He offered more nuance. First, he said, the phrase is true. Life is hard, but no matter how difficult today is, there will be a worse one ahead. There are two ways to look at that absolute truth. You can look ahead with fear or you can celebrate the best parts of today. "Cheer up, it gets worse," is not negative, he said. It is a reminder not to wallow in your troubles today because there will be a day in the future you will want to trade for today. Truly, an amazing piece of advice.

The other revelation was even more Warrior like. "Besides, when those two gals came into the store looking for you, I told them where you were. I said, 'don't linger long; he's working and the faster he gets done, the more it benefits everyone. Besides, the customer probably doesn't want a bunch of unexpected folks showing up at their house. I know I wouldn't.'" My dad probably put the fear of God into them. The reason they didn't spend more than five minutes with me was simple: they were following my father's instructions.

"Why didn't you tell me that back then?" I asked. He just shrugged, but I now know why. As a Warrior, it would have served no point. The desired outcomes were all achieved. Service call completed, yearbook photos taken. Check and check. The rest was just superfluous and unnecessary noise. There is no spot on a scoreboard for "other interesting details."

A WARRIOR IS A WINE'S TANNIN

Since Warriors value winning, displaying their status as winners is something they are quite comfortable with. They like the trophy. Arguably, the two biggest "trophy" wines are Napa and Bordeaux red wines. In both regions, Cabernet Sauvignon plays a vital role. One of the distinguishing characteristics of Cabernet Sauvignon is tannins, the astringent taste contributed by the grape skin, seeds, and stems. That's why tannins are more associated with red wines than white wines. Tannins give the wine more color, more dryness, and more aging ability. *More* is a good word for a Warrior.

My wine personality pairing for a Warrior is always Cabernet Sauvignon. The obvious choice would be a Napa cult Cabernet Sauvignon or a first growth, left bank red Bordeaux – which will have more Cabernet Sauvignon in the blend than the other grapes from the region. But that's too easy. Warriors like the best, for sure, but they also like to consider value. Anyone can buy an expensive bottle of trophy wine. But is that really *winning*? No; the better choice for the Warrior is to find an amazing bottle of Cabernet Sauvignon for an affordable price. *That* is winning. For the Warrior, it is not just about getting the right result; but doing so faster or cheaper than the competition.

As you did with the other assessment results, take some time to consider the influence of the Warrior style on your Me. If your score is below 30, the need to reach a result is part of your orientation and will influence how you approach situations and people. If your score is above 30, the influence of logic is less powerful. What does that mean? How has a relative lower preference for pushing toward a result manifested in your approach to life?

Spend a little time reflecting on what your Warrior column score might mean relative to your core ideology.

Up until now, we have evaluated your core ideology in the vacuum of the individual interactive styles. The mind, however, doesn't work that way. Just as every bottle of fine wine must achieve an effective balance of acidity, sweetness, fruit, and tannins, so must we. Our true self possesses a complexity that extends well beyond the singular focus on one style. Next, we will endeavor to examine the totality of our style preferences in our continuing odyssey to extract Me. Although our primary interactive style preference is the most informing of our overall style, the identification of the secondary preference and how it interplays with your primary preference adds this complexity. After all, human beings are not varietal wines. We are blends.

There is a large value to reading about each of the style combinations and not just your own. You will discover more nuance by doing so which will make your own interpretation of your scores even more effective. If you choose to skip to your own style, be sure to read Chapter 15, "Punching Down Your Own Style." This will provide you with a guided process for making the most of your exercise in metacognition.

PART THREE
THE BALANCE

Chapter 10 Punching Down the Cap

The Pursuit of Balance

> Give me books, French wine, fruit, fine weather,
> and a little music played out of doors
> by someone I do not know.
>
> – *John Keats*

We've come a long way. By now, you have explored your core ideology – including your vision, mission, and core values. You have started the process of understanding your style. If you have been documenting each of these activities, you now have an impressive journal of information that reflects much of your innermost nature. However, just like those many trips to the library to deepen your research into a topic, we still have a distance to go to truly extract Me.

In Part Two, we began the exploration of how our interactive style informs our true self. For some readers, this process began several years ago when they read my previous book, *The Power of Understanding People*. In that book, I explored the 12 iconic interactive styles by comparing them to famous characters in film and television. The purpose in that book was to better understand how to lead, sell to, provide service for, and develop better relationships with *other* people. This book takes things one step further by helping us determine, in an even deeper way, how to develop a better relationship with *ourselves*. Examining the complexities of our interactive styles is analogous for the vintner's efforts at achieving balance in a wine. Each bottle is a combination of acidity, sweetness/alcohol, fruit and tannins. To be completely accurate, sweetness and alcohol are two separate components; but since I link both to Romantics in my analogy, I have taken a wee bit of creative license. (Hey, it's my book.) Anyway, a winemaker's general goal is to bring those four components together in a balance that yields a distinctive and appealing final product. The same can be said about how the four interactive styles combine for us.

FINDING THE RIGHT BALANCE

In the preceding chapters, we learned about each of the four styles individually: Experts, Romantics, Masterminds, and Warriors. When it comes to transactional relationships – interactions with people who are providing us with service or for whom we are providing service, casual conversations with strangers, and even some coworkers – our primary style is the most important. However, to truly understand ourselves, we must consider how all four of our style preferences form our unique "balance." By doing so, we achieve a far greater understanding of our own perspective, our tendencies, and our blind spots. Knowing our inclinations, for better *and* for worse, is a critical piece of metacognition. Remember, our goal is to be fully aware of our selves – not just our gifts, but our vulnerabilities.

Unlike the vintner, our goal is not to achieve exact balance. Whereas wine may aspire to being perfect, human beings should not. Absolute balance in a human being is often viewed as unappealing in that it conceals the very flaws that define us. Unlike wine, a person's character lies in his or her imperfections. That is the beauty of the human condition. In that way, wine does provide us with a template to understand the value of imperfections. Unless you happen to have an incredible amount of disposable income – or a very unusual way of prioritizing your finances – you probably don't spend hundreds of dollars on each bottle of wine you purchase. Most of us consume wines that cost under $20.00 per bottle. At that price, the wine we are drinking can be very good, but will likely not achieve anything close to perfection. Although winemakers may endeavor to make a perfectly balanced bottle of wine, most of us learn to appreciate the remarkable complexities of slightly off-balanced creations. The same is true about the human experience.

The following chapters may require multiple reading and careful metacognition as you extract as much from your style assessment as possible. Also, be mindful of the content from Chapter 5, "What's My Style?," where we covered the concepts of dynamic, common, and nuanced patterns, as well as tie scores. It is impossible for me to clearly articulate all the possible combinations of your four interactive style preferences while also comprehensively addressing the nature of your pattern. If you consider that there are 24 permutations of the style assessment and add that these permutations can be dynamic, common, or nuanced, we are at 72 distinct patterns. Then, if you consider that a significant number of people will report out a tie in two (or more) of the columns . . . well, let's just say it would take someone with an Expert score around 12 to take on that task. My score was 37, so . . . yeah.

However, and in my opinion far more valuable, I *can* educate you on how to interpret your own results. That is the goal of the next chapters. You will find an explanation of your secondary style preference on your primary style preference.

Further, for each of the 12 combinations (three different secondary preferences that can exist for each of the four primary preferences) we will examine three areas:

1. Complementary versus contrasting balance
2. Preferences versus vulnerabilities
3. Impact on resiliency

Here's why each of these topics are important, starting with "complementary versus contrasting balance." This analysis revolves around the relationship between your primary (lowest score) style and your secondary (next lowest) style. Although there exist no opposites in style preference – despite the insistence of some assessment tools to display results in quadrants – there are certainly styles that are radically different. The Expert style, with its sensitivity to facts and desire to avoid mistakes, is quite divergent from the Mastermind's acceptance of possibilities and risk. The Romantic style of consensus building and tactful dialogue is markedly distinct from the Warrior's directness and focus on results. If your primary and secondary styles include these disparate components – Expert and Mastermind or Romantic and Warrior – then you are working with a contrasting balance. If your primary and secondary style do not combine the diverse elements, then you have a complementary balance. The details of this will be explained in the following chapters.

Although the examples in the preceding paragraph offer the most obvious contrasting balance dynamics, all combinations of primary and secondary preferences can create meaningful considerations. We will examine this impact for each of the 12 styles.

Preferences versus vulnerabilities is another important consideration when involved in metacognition. Interactive style acts as a filter for reality in many ways. It is obvious if you think about it. If you are emotionally sensitive, like the Romantic, then you notice the feelings in other people and the environment at large. This sensitivity gives rise to preferences within your surrounds and influences your behaviors. This can make you especially adept at certain things, unnecessarily responsive to certain things, and completely unaware of yet other things. The better we understand how we construct our personal delusion and the ramifications of that, the more we can make use of our gifts – and minimize our peccadilloes.

Finally, we will explore the influence that our interactive style has on resiliency. To evaluate this, let's first begin by defining resilience for the purposes of this book. Remember the stew story in Chapter 2, "It's Your Fault"? We know that life will eventually confront us with unpleasant circumstances. That is inevitable. Resiliency is our ability to respond to these events in a constructive way and return to a healthy orientation with a minimal toxic impact on our physical, mental, and emotional well being. A large part of resiliency is reaching a better understanding the role stress plays in our lives. Whereas the symptoms of stress can be well defined, the cause of stress and our means of coping versus strategies for successfully managing stress are more personal. Our ability to identify stress triggers and execute effective strategies for responding to, even preventing, stress is essential to our resilency. Our conversation on internal locus of control provides the foundation for achieving that goal.

THE GOOD AND BAD OF STRESS

Understanding our own response to stress and our strategy for maintaining resiliency is an important consideration when extracting me. It is helpful to realize here that stress is not an inherently bad thing. In fact, when used correctly, stress serves as our fuel for peak performance. Sudden stress, the influence of cortisol and adrenaline on our physicality, keeps us alive when we are threatened. Nerves, the jitters, butterflies in the stomach – all of these physical manifestations of sudden stress are indications that our bodies are preparing to perform at their best ability. In this way, the body's sudden response to a challenge and quick return to a relaxed state is the embodiment of resiliency. Unfortunately, many of our stress triggers are not easily nor quickly resolved.

The enemy is not sudden stress, but rather *chronic* stress – which occurs when we place a protracted period of duress on the body. If sudden stress reflects the load that our body can withstand in the near term, chronic stress is the overload – an unsustainable level of duress that is unrelenting for a longer period of time. Sudden stress is a natural reaction to a real or perceived threat. Chronic stress is a toxic reaction to a real or imagined threat. To illustrate, when I am clearing out tumble-weeds from a pasture and come across a snake, I experience sudden stress. My heart rate goes up, my cognitive focus narrows, and my behavioral reactions go on automatic pilot. I also tend to leap in the air and run about 50 yards, but the exact physical response varies by individual. Conversely, when I find myself repeatedly lying in bed worrying about the possibility that a future training event may go poorly, an event that is weeks in the future, I am experiencing chronic stress – a toxic reaction to an imagined threat. Finally, if I were to receive a dire health diagnosis or devastating financial news that results in my constant worry, that is chronic stress related to a real threat. Our style preferences can indicate the type of situations that can lead to chronic stress.

Understanding, managing, and utilizing stress has been a personal crusade for many years. For reasons that I will explain in a future chapter, I have had my own battles with chronic stress. Although that war may never end, I have reached a comfortable détente using metacognition to armor myself from my own tendencies. Stress comes from within, so any solution for the stress in your life must also. Each person has a unique combination of stress triggers, many of which can be identified by examining their interactive style pattern. Although stress plays an important, and often positive, role in our lives, it also has the potential for devastating impact on our health and well being. Any exploration of ourselves must include an examination of the role stress plays. Interestingly, winemakers prefer grapes that have experienced some stress to reach maturity.

As the German philosopher Friedrich Nietzsche said, "That which does not kill us, makes us stronger." Although I am not ready to test that theory in a literal sense, there is no question that our struggle can make us better, just as it does for the grapes.

A vintner uses more than just the grape juice to make a balanced and complex red wine. The stems, seeds, and skin separate from the juice and form a cap that sits on top of the wine. Without forcing that material back into juice, the wine can become thin and nondescript and is susceptible to bacteria that can make the wine flawed. The vintner must occasionally push the cap back into the wine to mix with juice. This activity is called the punch down. As the name suggests, it is a physical process of breaking up the cap and forcing it into juice for the benefit of the wine.

The next several chapters represent your punch down. It might be challenging, but it is essential to achieving a full, balanced, and complex extraction of Me.

Chapter 11 Punching Down the Expert Style Influence on Me

Wine is like many of the fine experiences in life which take time and experience to extract their full pleasure and meaning.

– Douglas Preston, Crimson Shore

Other people shape you. They shape you through mentoring and malice. They shape you by their behaviors and their beliefs. And they shape you through complement and contrast. As we understand more about Experts, here's my story of an unlikely mentor.

In the spring of 2015, I lost my mind. It wasn't the first time. In fact, I lose my mind quite frequently. There was that time in 1983 after I left a burgeoning career in broadcasting because I didn't enjoy it. I was 22 years old and already a producer for the local CBS network's television news show. In just under a year, I had moved from remote reporter to the head spot on the 10:00 p.m. newscast. Now, it was Terre Haute, Indiana, so

I was a long way from threatening Dan Rather's seat; but I was off to a fast start. But, I lost my mind, marched into the news director's office and quit. When I told my dad what I did, it went like this:

"Dad, I quit my job yesterday."

"Why the hell did you do that?" I am sure Dad had a vision of me moving back home flash in front of his eyes.

"I didn't enjoy it."

"Of course you didn't enjoy it. It's called *work*. That's why they pay you. If you enjoyed it, you would have to pay them." <Muttering> "'Didn't enjoy it,' Christ. I didn't enjoy the Depression, but I was damn glad when I had work. You ever eat a jam sandwich? I have. That's two pieces of bread jammed together with nothing between it. And I was happy to have it. 'Didn't enjoy it.' What in Sam Hill is that?"

Two takeaways: First, Dad wasn't much for the whole "find your gift" era of career counseling. Second, who is this Sam Hill fella? Dad referred to him a lot, generally when he was mad. I never met Sam Hill, but I am pretty sure that he is not a pleasant person.

My episodic insanity flared again in 1990. My lovely bride was pregnant with our first child, and I was a successful human resources leader at Marshall Field's, a large department store chain in Chicago, Illinois. From the outside looking in, our life was a perfect yuppy suburban success story. But, I wasn't happy. I spent my workdays driving to a train station, taking the train into the city, catching a bus to the office, working 8–10 hours, then reversing course. My workday started at 5:00 a.m. and ended at 7:30 p.m. Like most people who live in the suburbs and work in the city, I was part of that walking dead horde that packed the trains. I wanted more time with my family. More time doing the things I loved. I *liked* work, but I didn't enjoy it.

There was the weather, too. My God, Chicago weather sucks. It's such a great city with so many fantastic people and exactly four nice days each year. The rest are windy, hot, humid, cold, snowy, and cloudy. And walking across the Chicago river? Well, I am pretty sure there is a mortality rate associated with that travail, a carefully guarded secret among members of the Chamber of Commerce.

So, I quit. I quit and moved. I moved to Orlando, Florida to pursue a human resources career with Walt Disney World. It was not a smooth transition. Who would have guessed that suddenly moving more than 1,000 miles away without selling your home or having a job would be challenging? Oh, and did I mention that my lovely bride was pregnant? Like *really* pregnant? Like, we moved in April and Brooke was born in May, pregnant? Yep, insane.

Clearly, losing my mind from time to time is something I do. I have noticed that it happens in the spring. It may be allergies. Anyway, in spring of 2015 we decided to move from our idyllic home in the mountains of Colorado where we had spent 14 years developing friendships, raising our kids, and learning how to navigate life in the mountains and head to wine country. We bought a house on 20 acres of land outside Walla Walla, Washington. Twenty acres of land that would require *a lot* of maintenance. I had clearly, once again, lost my mind.

The most notable early lesson was that our land was under constant attack by the Russians. Unlike the clandestine actions Russians were taking against our social media channels, this attack was not covert. Oh no – this was an obvious, visible, and malicious assault by a particularly malevolent type of Russian: the Russian Thistle and its sinister weapon – the tumbleweed.

I hope scientists who are searching for the secret to eternal life are investing copious amounts of time studying the Russian Thistle. By my calculations, it is impervious to every single conventional weed killing strategy known to human kind. You know those substances with labels that warn you that merely uttering the name of the active ingredient in the herbicide may cause cancer? Russian Thistle just giggles when you spray it. If you try pulling them, they will turn your hand into a bloody stump. Even hitting them with a propane torch generates mixed results. This plant is *badass*. If I ever become an agent for the CIA, my code name will be Russian Thistle.

Finally, in the summer of 2017, I called for backup. I decided I would re-structure my entire backyard, about an acre of land, into a beautifully landscaped fire pit and rock-covered oasis. No grass and no weeds. No Russian Thistle. It was my scorched Earth Russian Thistle strategy. Total annihilation. For a plan as bold as this, I would need an Expert – and that Expert was Adrian.

From May until September 2017, Adrian and I spent several days each week – those days when I was not out of town on speaking engagements – digging, measuring, putting in landscaping fabric, digging, moving dirt, shoveling rocks, digging, installing walkways, laying tiles – oh, and did I mention that we also dug? I lost 20 pounds in just over four months.

Most notably, I experienced the incredible gift that is the Expert style. Adrian would measure everything repeatedly. Every part of our yard was level—the fire pit walls, floor, the ground around it, the walkways to and from it. Every time I was ready to take a shortcut, to succumb to my Warrior need to just be *done*, Adrian would reel me back in and check our work. I would be lying if I told you that it wasn't frustrating for me. The final product, however, is a constant reminder of how valuable Expert thinking can be. My vulnerability, with an Expert score of 37, is that I don't pay close attention to details. My desire to get a result puts pressure on taking time to ensure quality. Adrian provided the contrast to my style. He was my mentor.

COMPLEMENTARY VERSUS CONTRASTING BALANCE

If you are an Expert – meaning that your lowest scoring column is A – you are also influenced by one of the remaining three columns. Your second lowest score – your secondary preference – provides your complementary balance. Although it is not your *preferred* style, it exerts significant influence on your approach and response to life. This is particularly true if your second preference score is below 30. If your secondary preference scores about 30, then it has a slightly more muted influence over your style. Whereas most people will report a clear secondary preference, there are a significant number of people who have only one column with a score below 30. This is most likely the result of a dynamic pattern (see Chapter 5, "What's My Style"). In these cases, the primary preference is so strong that it dominates the other style preferences.

The other situation that results in only one score below 30 is a nuanced pattern, also described in Chapter 5. Unlike the dynamic pattern, the nuanced pattern is influenced by three or all four of the interactive style preferences. If your patterns do not fall into an obvious primary and secondary preference representation, this would be a good time to re-read Chapter 5, "What's My Style?," to consider the impact of your pattern of preference on your true self. The rest of the following four chapters examining each style preference will focus on a common pattern result to the assessment tool.

AN EXPERT WITH A SECONDARY ROMANTIC (LOWEST SCORE A COLUMN, NEXT-LOWEST SCORE B COLUMN)

We all have our strengths and vulnerabilities. The more we understand the impact of both, the better we can utilize them to be the best Me we can be. As explained earlier, Experts tend to be thorough, detailed, accurate, risk avoidant and serious in their pursuit of perfection. All these qualities are immensely important in many life pursuits. Had I not experienced Adrian's leadership during my landscaping adventure, I am certain that the county would have condemned my entire backyard within months. However, the same perspective that makes Experts so important to achieving a quality result can also make them appear stubborn, resistant to change, overly cautious, and stuck in the minutia of policies, procedures, and best practices.

A secondary preference for the Romantic style helps the Expert become more attuned to the emotional reaction they are receiving. That secondary style preference adds diplomacy, tact, empathy and political awareness to their viewpoint.

Although the Expert will always prefer to approach tasks with their own knowledge and experience as their guide, the secondary Romantic style allows them more room for consensus building, input, and discussion. In my previous book, I refer to this style as the Voice of Reason. The combination of a primary Expert, secondary Romantic style often reflects outwardly as a teacher or mentor. They exude knowledge, patience, and professionalism. Although they may have a dogged determination to enforce accuracy and compliance, they can soften that expectation with delicacy and consideration.

I am fond of saying that the Voice of Reason cares deeply about others and displays that orientation by providing education to keep them out of harm's way. I am most impressed by the Voice of Reason's ability to hold people accountable for doing the right thing without making them feel degraded or scolded. Although I do not subscribe to the belief that a person's style should guide their vocational choice, I do find that the Voice of Reason people are excellent teachers, combining the desire for best practices with the preference for tact and diplomacy. It is also important for me to note that "doing the right thing" is not a values statement. For the Expert, doing the right thing is a reference to doing the thing that we know produces the desired result. Style and values are two different components of self.

The Voice of Reason people have two contrasting balance components: Mastermind and Warrior. Understanding your contrasting balance gives you a better understanding of your vulnerabilities. A high score (above 30) in the Mastermind (C) column reduces your willingness to take risk. It can also restrict your interest and orientation to concepts, ideas, and possibilities. It would be beneficial to an Expert with a contrasting high Mastermind score to be aware of their tendency to be suspicious of situations, thoughts, proposals, and – possibly – even people for whom they have little or no experience or information. Although these new opportunities may cause some duress for an Expert, embracing them in the face of the risk can help them expand their knowledge. Just as the Expert perspective can add tremendous value to a new idea, a Master-mind perspective can help shove an individual who resists risk into a wonderful new direction.

Another contrasting balance consideration for the Voice of Reason is a score about 30 in the Warrior (D) column. At the risk of oversimplifying this contrast, if the Expert style is about quality, the Warrior style is about quantity. One of the fundamental challenges of most businesses is balancing the quality of the products and services with the quantity sold. There is nearly always a struggle to maintain both. Voice of Reason people may benefit by appreciating that the pressure to produce and to reach a result rivals their own need to be accurate. This contrasting balance is often a key cultural challenge within organizations between sales and operations – sales being measured by production (Warrior), operations by customer satisfaction (Expert).

I witnessed this friction at Mitchell's Heating and Air Conditioning, the small business owned by my Warrior father. Generally, my father would spend his time selling. He would stay in the showroom to sell appliances or travel to job sites to bid on HVAC projects. Each morning, however, he assigned the three or four repair/installation professionals their service calls for the day. I would watch him as he grew increasingly frustrated with the many questions they would have about the calls. All the questions were legitimate, particularly to an Expert; but in my Dad's view, it was wasting time. "Do something even if it's wrong," was a common retort from Dale. Translated, Dad was saying, "Jesus Christ, I could have driven there, figured it out, fixed it, and been back in the time we have talked about it."

Of course, on those occasions when my Dad had to go out and do the service work himself, I would also hear him utter the phrase, "Good enough for who it's for." Now, to defend my father, he was self-aware of his tendency to get things working, but not necessarily do things right. He would send a service man back out to finish his work the correct way. My Dad's goal was to get an appliance working again, not fix it the best way. He prioritized speed over accuracy. Taken to an extreme, that would create quality problems. However, the alternative created financial problems. Therein lies the dilemma of quantity versus quality, Warrior versus Expert.

An Expert with a contrasting balance of a high score in the Warrior column can benefit by understanding the importance of productivity. Learning to evaluate the relative merits of the pursuit of perfection against the value of a result will help the Voice of Reason people achieve a fuller perspective.

Finally, how does this score impact resiliency? As a reminder, an internal locus of control is the foundation for resiliency and is unrelated to interactive style. However, our intrinsic needs are also valuable for insulating us from chronic stress. The Voice of Reason excels in environments that feel secure, reliable, consistent, and within which they are appreciated for their knowledge and expertise. This style is generally not prone to flamboyance, preferring the steady and unassuming approach to excellence over flagrant displays of contribution. For this reason, their contribution can be overlooked or taken for granted – a situation that can leave them susceptible to chronic stress.

The Voice of Reason people may also encounter potential for chronic stress in situations that are not sufficiently *structured*. Like all Experts, the Voice of Reason people do not respond well to sustained chaotic environments. Time pressure can also be detrimental to the stress state of this style. Demands for greater productivity can negatively impact quality, an untenable situation for Voice of Reason people. Being told to "get it done now" versus "get it done right" will cause chronic stress.

If you score as a Voice of Reason person, take care to ensure that you have sufficient sources for personal appreciation and stability in your life. These components will help armor you against the derogatory effects of chronic stress. Table 11.1 gives a short summary of the Voice of Reason style.

Table 11.1   The Voice of Reason Punch Down

Complementary Versus Contrasting Balance	Preferences Versus Vulnerabilities	Impact on Resiliency
• Primary style = Expert • Complementary Style = Romantic • Contrasting Styles = Mastermind and Warrior	• Prefers structured, secure situations that can benefit the well-being and emotions of others. • May avoid situations that they view as too risky. • May sacrifice productivity for the sake of quality.	• Responds well to environments that are reliable and safe. • Thrives when being appreciated and respected for their knowledge • May experience chronic stress when forced to take chances or is the subject of extreme time pressure.

AN EXPERT WITH A SECONDARY MASTERMIND (LOWEST SCORE A COLUMN, NEXT-LOWEST SCORE C COLUMN)

Those of us who have been exposed to interactive style preference assessments – which is practically everyone – have grown comfortable with the quadrant approach. This application characterizes individuals as either conceptual or factual – an Expert or a Mastermind. However, it has been my experience that one can be influenced by both facts and ideas. This is one of the primary differentiators of my assessment. An Expert with a secondary Mastermind lives in both the world of the known and the unknown.

I refer to this style as the Detective. A detective must determine the unknown by pursuing what is known. The search for clues will yield a greater understanding of things that we do not currently understand. This person is the consummate researcher, compulsively sifting through data to piece together the information necessary to determine what has yet to be discovered.

Adrian, the star of my landscaping story, strikes me as a Detective. He combines a rigid commitment to quality with a substantial level of risk tolerance. Not only is he an entrepreneur; he also eagerly accepts projects for which he has little experience but will research thoroughly to understand. These are some of the common qualities of the Detective – an uncommon commitment to quality combined with a significant risk acceptance. If this sounds like you, that interesting paradox may well inform your style. I think that the Detective provides an extremely valuable perspective to any sort change – both personal and organizational. Their secondary Mastermind style makes them open, even eager, to accept new ideas and ways of doing things, while their primary Expert style will quickly recognize the structural, procedural and pragmatic challenges that may be involved. If I were assembling a team to implement change, I would start with the Detective.

Although the rigidity associated with many Experts may be less overt in the Detective, there are other potential vulnerabilities that exist in the contrasting balance. Detectives are not renowned for their tact and diplomacy. They are often depicted in movies and television shows as being interesting – even sometimes neurotic – loners who solve crimes, health challenges or global crisis with their expertise. Think Columbo, Sherlock Homes, Monk, and Iron Man. Sheldon on *The Big Bang Theory* is a great example. In all these cases, the lack of the Romantic preference is essential to the characters. They are not mean or brusque so much as matter of fact and oblivious to how their statements may land on the emotions of others.

As with the Voice of Reason people, Detectives may also struggle to balance their desire for quality and thoroughness with the need for a result. The relative lack of the contrasting Warrior style can remove the pressure of time. Here's an example:

My brother-in-law Russ is a Detective. Before retiring, Russ worked in a segment of technology that was rapidly becoming outdated and extinct, but many of his clients tried to postpone investing in expensive new equipment. His knowledge of the equipment was unparalleled, and he was fearless in finding new ways to deal with challenges of aging technology and equipment in his efforts to keep his clients happy. He would literally *invent processes* that kept these older products functional. Although Russ and I were as different as two people can be from an interactive style perspective, we shared a love for music, wine, and the occasional cigar. We spent many an evening sitting by his pool in Central Florida contemplating the mysteries of the universe while listening to some wonderful blues, jazz, or rock.

We also shared a love for high fidelity. High-end audiophile enthusiasts understand that this is a hobby that can get expensive. We enthusiasts tend to fall into two categories, (1) save your money and spend it on really cool equipment that you will listen to a lot because you now have no money to do anything else or (2) build your own. I was a category 1 audiophile. Russ was a category 2. For years, Russ would talk about building some amazing floor speakers. For another several years, Russ researched how to build some amazing floor speakers. Then, finally, Russ built some amazing floor speakers. The entire process lasted a decade. No Warrior in human history would have contemplated and researched a process for that long without a result.

The Detective's resiliency is based on both security and excitement. A consistent, reliable, and well-structured life will be great for some periods of time, but they also need the occasional project. The project will eventually become structured, reliable, and consistent and give way to the next project. Adrian is a great example of this. His landscaping business could be successful based on weekly mowing clients alone. Arguably, the business model is less risky and easier to execute. But for Adrian, the thought of doing nothing but rudimentary landscaping does not offer the entire recipe for his resiliency. He needs to mix the foundation of security with the excitement of new projects. Conversely, new projects alone would create too much potential chaos in his life.

The Detective may experience greater stress when forced into situations that require consensus, diplomacy, and the navigation of organizational politics. Perhaps that is why they are depicted as loners. Finally, like their colleague, the Voice of Reason, applying time pressure on the Detective can risk chronic stress. Although Detectives are among the world's great problem solvers, (it's elementary, my dear Watson!), they prefer to work in a methodical way. Rushing a Detective can risk poor quality or inadequate ideas. Table 11.2 gives a short summary of the Detective style.

Table 11.2   The Detective Punch Down

Complementary Versus Contrasting Balance	Preferences Versus Vulnerabilities	Impact on Resiliency
• Primary style = Expert • Complementary Style = Mastermind • Contrasting Styles = Romantic and Warrior	• Seeks depth of knowledge and will apply it creatively. • Researches thoroughly before taking chances. • May be a bit quirky or interpersonally clunky.	• Responds well to environments that are reliable and safe. • Likes freedom to invent and experiment • May experience chronic stress when dealing with social situations or extreme time pressure.

AN EXPERT WITH A SECONDARY WARRIOR (LOWEST SCORE A COLUMN, NEXT-LOWEST SCORE D COLUMN)

One of the cognitive struggles that is common to most people is the balance of the pursuit of perfection with the desire to be *done*. I believe that we all exist along this continuum. For me, the desire to be done is stronger than the pursuit of perfection. For my friend Adrian, it is the opposite. That is why we work well together. I apply the time pressure; he ensures the quality. But for some people, the search for this balance is a particularly defining characteristic. Such is the case for the Specialist.

The addition of a secondary Warrior style creates a heightened awareness of time/value ratio. The Expert style alone does not place a time limit on the value of accuracy. With a secondary Warrior, now the Expert faces a finite period within which to pursue perfection. Things must be done right *and* on time. Driven by both quality and deadlines, the Specialist is the closest to a perfectionist of any of the twelve combinations of styles.

I have done seminars with many project management teams over my career. Learning to understand how people think, what motivates them and how to best communicate with a wide range of team members is especially valuable to professionals who are responsible for managing a work product that spans many types of contributors and contributions. With the caveat that any style can succeed in any job, provided the organization supports that approach, the most common pattern I have experienced for project management in the construction industry is the Specialist. It makes perfect sense.

For example – taking a very macro view, the success of a construction project hinges on three elements: quality of work, adherence to budget, and on-time completion. Given all the "moving parts" that are involved in, say, the building of a high rise, achieving those three elements is no small order. The successful project manager will require an attention to detail, unwavering commitment to quality, and will continually manage the pace of process to ensure timely delivery of the final product. This plays particularly well to the Specialist's strengths. Specialists are the cognitive embodiment of kaizen – a Japanese term used by business to mean "continuous improvement."

Although Specialists are often driven to perfection, their lower preferences for Romantic and Mastermind styles can create some challenges. The high Romantic score (low preference) combined with the urgency of a low Warrior Score (high preference) can conspire to reduce communication to "need to know" directives. Specialists can sometimes appear overly task focused. They can tend to be hypercritical, given that perfection that meets deadlines leaves little room for variance in the expectations of this style.

The high Mastermind score (low preference) also may limit flexibility. Again, a project manager trying to do things right, on time, and on budget won't want to "experiment" with new ideas midstream. The Specialist style is known for the quality and timeliness of the result—not how creative it is or if everyone enjoyed the process.

There are specific style combinations that pose the biggest challenge to resiliency. The Specialist is one of these patterns. Because of the natural tension between quality and quantity, people who value both are likely to struggle to find a balance. It is important for Specialists to feel secure and independent. Proper training, thorough communication, consistent and dependable situations are all important to their success. Also, the ability to apply their impressive knowledge in an environment that is free from micromanagement will be important. Too much time spent in meetings, engaged in "unproductive activities" like socializing, conference calls, or red tape will create stress. Likewise, chaotic, unpredictable, or poorly structured environments can create excessive duress for Specialists. Table 11.3 gives a short summary of the Specialist style.

Table 11.3   The Specialist Punch Down

Complementary Versus Contrasting Balance	Preferences Versus Vulnerabilities	Impact on Resiliency
• Primary style = Expert • Complementary Style = Warrior • Contrasting Styles = Mastermind and Romantic	• Prefers structured, efficient situations. • Perfectionist who doesn't suffer fools gladly. • May seem resistant to change and intolerant of mistakes.	• Responds well to training and structure. • Thrives on independence to do things their way. • May experience chronic stress when forced to take chances or build consensus with others.

EXTRACTING ME WORKSHEET

Take some time to complete the What's My Style? section of your worksheet. Since you are an Expert, I expect this to be thorough and detailed! And remember: there are no right answers, so don't overanalyze this. Take time to consider how your style preferences contribute to whom you are. Also consider how the styles that are not your primary or secondary preferences affect who you are. Remember, the most obvious component of who we are in the minds of others is our style. Since I know you like resources and are good with research, check out Chapter 15 for an example of punching down your style.

Chapter 12 Punching Down the Romantic Style Influence on Me

I love everything that is old; old friends, old times, old manners, old books, old wines.

– Oliver Goldsmith

My first career aspiration was to be the first baseman for the New York Mets. It was a path that I pursued enthusiastically through high school with modest success. Like thousands of other kids, I was a pretty good baseball player. Unfortunately, after my senior year of high school, it became clear I suffered from a debilitating condition – insufficient talent. This condition was compounded by some important physical limitations. First, I was 5'11", weighed 175 pounds, and had hit exactly four home runs after the age of 15. Generally, teams view the first baseman as a power hitter, so my ability to ground out to the second baseman was not coveted. Perhaps a move to shortstop or second base might have better matched my hitting skills; but I am also left-handed.

In baseball, left-handers are generally relegated to the outfield, first base, or pitching. Outfielders usually fall into two categories: power hitters or speedsters. We have established my power. As a baserunner, I was told I had "good instincts." "Good instincts" on the bases is code for "runs like he is carrying a piano."

"Pitcher!" was the enthusiastic solution offered by one of my coaches before he discovered that I was not "warming up"; that was my fastball. When that ever-optimistic coach asked me what other pitches I threw, I told him that I could vary the speed of my pitches.

"So, you can throw even slower?" The coach was clearly impressed that my fastball wasn't my slowest pitch. Unfortunately, throwing progressively slower is not considered useful to your team. The other team, yes. Not your team.

So, my baseball career transitioned to slow pitch softball before joining my basketball and football career in retirement. And while I never fulfilled my dream of playing first base for the New York Mets, I did experience the coaching techniques of many people from T-Ball to American Legion. All of these coaches imparted wisdom – some because of their sports acumen, others for their qualities as a human being. Dave Decker fell in the latter category.

Coach Decker was a teacher, not just of sports but also of science. Literally. Like so many high school coaches, Mr. Decker was involved in the sport both because of a love of education and youth and the desire to augment his teaching salary. I liked Mr. Decker the science teacher. I *loved* Coach Decker. He was unlike any coach I would ever have.

Nearly all my coaches, regardless of sport, were yellers. Yellers use decibels to get your attention. It is a proven strategy in athletics and I am certainly not going to argue its merits. Yellers also seem to be very critical of players. Truth be told, they are probably no more critical than nonyellers. But when the yellers criticize you, everyone in the gym, on the field, heck, in the general vicinity, know you have been criticized. Many players respond quite well to yellers. Me, not so much.

Coach Decker was the first coach I played for who was not a yeller. Coach Decker approached coaching like he approached teaching. He was patient. He explained things. He maintained a calm, steady demeanor. He was tactful, caring, and empathetic. The season that I played with Coach Decker was my favorite baseball season. Coach Decker was a Romantic – and, like Adrian the Expert, he was another of my mentors.

It is interesting – for many reasons – that the season I played for Coach Decker, although my most enjoyable, was my least successful statistically. I had always been a good hitter, if lacking in power. The fact that I rarely struck out and had good strike-zone awareness meant that I hit for a high average and walked a lot. I could even steal a base here and there (remember, "good instincts on the bases"). Coach Decker installed me as the lead-off hitter, fully expecting those skills to payoff. Unfortunately, I started the season hitless in our first five games spanning nearly 20 at bats. Coach Decker, nonetheless, would write my name at the top of the lineup and continued to encourage me as I fought through my slump.

I am certain that any of my other coaches would have become frustrated with my lack of productivity, perhaps criticized me, and most certainly would have dropped me to the bottom of the lineup if not bench me altogether. Dave Decker did none of these things. Eventually, my hitting came around and while my final stats were hopelessly damaged by my early season struggles, my confidence was not. I learned that I responded best to being appreciated and encouraged. My Romantic preference was already fully formed even in my teens.

All Romantics want world peace; they just go about it in different ways depending on their secondary style preference. All Romantics also thrive in environments that are rich with appreciation. And, like all primary preferences, they are influenced by their second style.

A ROMANTIC WITH A SECONDARY EXPERT (LOWEST SCORE B COLUMN, SECOND-LOWEST SCORE A COLUMN)

Although tact, diplomacy, and situational awareness are all hallmarks of the Romantics, perhaps no pairing of styles is more cognizant of being appropriate than this combination of preferences. The marriage of emotional sensitivity with risk avoidance and security creates a mind that is fine-tuned to properness. You can make a very good case that this combination is the nicest – which is the reason I refer to the Romantic Expert as the Best Friend.

Given that the Best Friend combines an understanding of the emotional landscape and prefers fact-based, low-risk situations, they are often exceptional counselors of others. They are both patient and considerate, fantastic qualities in a listener. Similar in style to the previously discussed Voice of Reason, the Best Friend is more advisor than teacher, although they are well suited for both. Possessing both tact and patience is uncommon, and the two traits are often confused for each other. The Best Friend's empathy to others' feelings provides the origin for their tact. Their desire for reliable, accurate, and consistent processes is the foundation for their patience. Tactful people can be impatient, using their tact to conceal their irritation. Patient people can lack tact, relentlessly defending policies and standards in their quest for quality. The Best Friend displays both attributes.

As the name implies, Best Friends rarely apply pressure to others, preferring a shepherding-like approach to directing people. Getting things done correctly in a manner that does not create conflict with others is their preferred strategy. As with other Romantics, they are prone to self-sacrifice and can be susceptible to over extending themselves to avoid confrontations with others.

They also prefer familiar experiences, approaches, and processes. They are not known for innovation but can be very successful at installing structure to situations that are new.

Although Best Friends may not *introduce* radical change, they are often vital to reducing risk during periods of change through their ability to reassure others and orientation toward rules. They can mitigate the risk of big ideas by providing procedures to ensure quality outcomes.

The potential blind spots for Best Friends lie in the Warrior and Mastermind styles. These scores fall about the 30 mid-point. This can conspire to prolong the Best Friend's sense of urgency. A high score in column D (Warrior) can reduce the need to a result that is useful in balancing the need for quality. The high score in column C (Mastermind) creates the risk aversion that makes the Best Friend reluctant to be an early adopter of ideas and an initiator of change. These are areas to consider for the Best Friend when engaged in metacognition.

Finally, despite the reputation of the Best Friend for being the nicest of styles, they can be extremely protective of their circle. This is no more obvious than in their behavior with family. It is common for a Best Friend to expect loved ones to comply with very specific codes of conduct. I am reminded of an episode I witnessed at an appliance dealers showroom while doing some training on behalf of Electrolux.

A delightful couple with two young children walked into the store in the market for a new refrigerator. I was observing the sales dynamic as part of the preparation for my class on consultative selling. Based on the rigid behavior of the two children, roughly between the ages of 5 and 10, it seemed clear to me that there had been a "Come to Jesus" meeting in the car before entering the store. Since the Mom was the clear leader of the family, at least in this situation, I imagine she had convened the parking lot discussion. It probably went something like this.

"Okay, we are going into the store to look at refrigerators. There will be lots of interesting things in that store, but I need you to stay close to Mom the entire time and do not touch anything. Do you understand?" Mom would have said this with love but also with a firmness that let everyone in the car: Bobby, Billy, and even Dad, know that she expected unwavering compliance.

"Yes" they would have replied in unison.

Once inside the store, it was Mom who drove the process. As the salesperson approached, Mom explains their situation with all the sweetness one would expect from a Best Friend. "Hi, I'm Janet. This is my husband Robert and this is Bobby and Billy. We are looking for a refrigerator. The one we have is adorable, but it is getting a little outdated. It came with the house we bought 10 years ago and we have just outgrown it. It's perfectly fine but I feel like we need something a . . ."

Meanwhile, little Billy has wandered away from the family and touches something that makes a noise.

"BILLY, GET OVER HERE!" The sheer force and volume of Janet's voice rocks the showroom. Billy drops to the ground, as does Bobby, Robert and, perhaps, even the salesperson. Without missing a beat, Janet continues her context.

". . . so I'm not sure if we want a side-by-side model or a bottom-mount freezer . . ." Sweet Janet has returned.

Keep in mind, the shepherd carries a staff. The staff is not to whack wolves to protect the sheep. No, the staff is to nudge the sheep away from the wolves. Billy just got nudged.

The Best Friend's resiliency lies in feeling appreciated for their efforts to keep people safe. They are naturally altruistic and thrive when they know that others are aware of and value their sacrifice. They also do best when they are familiar with what is expected of them and others. Situations and environments that contain excessive pressure and chaos are particularly stressful for the Best Friend. Table 12.1 gives a short summary of the Best Friend style.

A ROMANTIC WITH A SECONDARY MASTERMIND (LOWEST SCORE B COLUMN, SECOND-LOWEST SCORE C COLUMN)

I must admit a lack of objectivity as it relates to this combination. My lovely bride's style falls into this category and I have noticed that many of my friends do, too; so I clearly have a special affinity for this style. And why not? They combine the

Table 12.1   The Best Friend Punch Down

Complementary Versus Contrasting Balance	Preferences Versus Vulnerabilities	Impact on Resiliency
• Primary style = Romantic • Complementary Style = Expert • Contrasting Styles = Mastermind and Warrior	• Excellent counselor who offers practical advice to benefit others. • Tends to self-sacrifice and avoid conflict. • Tactful, diplomatic and appropriate communicator.	• Responds well to genuine appreciation. • Responds well to environments that are reliable and safe. • Negative morale and chaotic environments are stressful.

emotional sensitivity of the Romantic style with the charm of the Mastermind style. They are the world's public relations and marketing person. Although their primary concern is tending to the feelings of others, they possess a degree of risk tolerance that makes them open to life's adventures. In this regard, their life can be much like the script from a romantic comedy and their role becomes the lead character – the Love Interest.

Replacing the second lowest score of the Best Friend of Expert with a secondary Mastermind relaxes the risk avoidance influence on the style. The Love Interest is more comfortable in loosely defined situations and willing to take some chances – as long as it doesn't make others uncomfortable. If the Best Friend is the epitome of nice, then the Love Interest is the poster child of fun. Given that the Love Interest prefers fun experiences without any emotional discomfort for others, it makes Love Interests that much more appealing.

One of the Love Interest's great gifts is their ability to get others excited about the possibilities. They are exceptional at messaging and are very valuable in selling ideas and changes to others who might be skeptical of the consequences. This medium runs both ways, too. Love Interests not only can promote ideas from one group to another but can close the feedback loop by taking the reaction to the ideas back to those that initiated it. In this regard, they are excellent communicators. And while their secondary Mastermind makes them comfortable and even excited about new ideas and experiences, they are just as supportive of others' ideas as they are their own.

The challenge for the Love Interest is in dealing with situations that are not fun, interesting, or conducive to positive emotional responses. Strict compliance to processes and procedures can "suck the fun" out of an experience. Also, pressure applied by deadlines can strip them of their ability to monitor the reaction to ideas. Drudgery is not particularly appealing to any style, but it is mortally undesirable to the Love Interest.

For example, my lovely bride Lori works as a wine-tasting-room manager in Walla Walla. As professions go, managing a beautiful wine-tasting room in a town known for being "so nice we named it twice" in the middle of a picturesque wine region is about as great as it gets. At least, *I* think so. I even volunteer to help from time to time because it really doesn't feel like work.

Having stated that, the process involved in a wine tasting is very structured. There is a specific order that the wines are poured in; there are legal requirements that guide and restrict your approach; and you repeat the same processes over and over and over. The only variable is the client. For a Love Interest, the work itself is not that appealing. It is the variety of clients that make the job interesting. The measure of Lori's day is less about the amount of sales or the accuracy of the operational controls but rather the number of cool people she got to meet and the new friends that she made. I am forever impressed by the number of people she knows – not just in Walla Walla, but from Seattle, Portland, Boise, and other visitors to the winery. With my style being Romantic/Warrior (see next section), the two questions I ask her when she gets home are: "How was your day? What were your sales?" What she wants to talk about is "Who did you meet?"

Table 12.2   The Love Interest Punch Down

Complementary Versus Contrasting Balance	Preferences Versus Vulnerabilities	Impact on Resiliency
• Primary style = Romantic • Complementary Style = Mastermind • Contrasting Styles = Expert and Warrior	• Loves to lift the spirits of those around them. • Likes new opportunities particularly if it makes others happy. • Conflict and boredom are demotivating.	• Enjoys environments that offer new experiences. • Does well when their charm is valued by others. • Restrictive and intense environments can be stressful.

So, the area of vulnerability for the Love Interest includes the things that don't offer them much fun: processes and deadlines. For the Love Interest to maximize their contribution, it may be necessary for them to comply with systems that ensure consistency and to have clear metrics to measure their progress.

Like the Best Friend, the Love Interest thrives in environments where they are appreciated. They, too, tend to sacrifice their own needs – and it is important that this not go unnoticed. But unlike the Best Friend, the Love Interest enjoys a more loosely organized environment where there is some freedom to customize the experience, make exceptions, and experience situations that are outside the norm. Table 12.2 gives a short summary of the Love Interest style.

A ROMANTIC WITH A SECONDARY WARRIOR (LOWEST SCORE B COLUMN, SECOND-LOWEST SCORE D COLUMN)

One of my favorite moments during my seminar on The Power of Understanding People is when I explain how Romantics come in three different styles. Romantics are one of the most common preferred styles in the United States, so as many as half my attendees can be in this one group when I have them stand if the B column is their lowest score. I quickly point out that they may be surprised to be standing along with someone else that they don't think is very similar to them in terms of style. It is then that I mention the influence of the secondary preference. The moment goes like this:

"You all share a primary Romantic style, but you may have different secondary styles. What this means is that you all prefer world peace, but you go about achieving it in different ways. The Romantic with a secondary A column preference gets world peace by providing security. The Romantic with a secondary C column preference gets world peace by providing possibilities . . ."

". . . And the Romantic with a secondary D column preference gets world peace by killing."

Immediately, the Crusaders understand their internal conflict.

Like all Romantics, the Crusader is keenly aware of the emotional content within their environment. Unlike the other types of Romantics, the Crusader feels a substantial amount of pressure to drive toward results. This pressure can often create conflict, confrontation, and discomfort – potentially negative and unpleasant feelings for the Crusader. Attempting to reconcile their desire to make others happy as well as their desire to efficiently reach closure is the core of the Crusader's style. Like most things related to the human condition, this dynamic reflects the Crusaders' blessing and their curse.

My dog Red, my frequent wander/ponder companion of my youth mentioned in the Preface of this book, was one of my first best friends. One of the things that I admired most about Red was his demeanor. He was fiercely loyal toward his family. He was kind and gentle until he perceived a threat to any of his loved ones. Then he would bark ferociously and convincingly display an attitude that indicated the capacity for extreme violence. Red never bit anyone, but he chased a few uninvited strangers out of our yard. He even treed one particularly shady salesperson.

It could well be that my affinity for Red was due in part to a form of style kinship. Red was a Crusader, like myself. It also could be that Red was a mentor for me. Perhaps it was the observance of Red's behavior that shaped my own. Whichever is true, Red embodied he Crusader style . . . that of peaceful warrior, righteous protector, the fighter for the cause.

Now, lest you think I am creating a very heroic narrative for this style, the Crusaders have their own plentiful vulnerabilities. For one, since they fight for causes, they can be difficult to reason with. If you believe you are doing something because it is "the right thing to do," then you are unlikely to be swayed by an opposing perspective. In fact, to compromise the cause would be fundamentally unappealing to the Crusader. And since they choose their fights for reasons that are not fiscal but based on virtue (as they define it) then they will fight to the death. Of course, I mean all of this metaphorically; but the truth remains that there have been no more bloody conflicts than those between Crusaders.

Crusaders care deeply and are called to action quickly. They are not likely to be bystanders; they prefer to do what is necessary to get their desired result for the good of those for whom they fight. Although they are often knowledgeable about the rules, they do exercise the ability to step outside the structure to achieve the goal. They also prefer efficiency to chaos and grow frustrated in environments that are not moving quickly to closure. Their contrasting styles of Mastermind and Expert create some discomfort for both new ideas and compliance to rules. They are more influenced by people and results.

Reconciling the desire for world peace with the pressure to achieve a specific outcome is the crux of their resilience battle. It can be very hard to win *and* be liked, the two intrinsic needs of the Crusader. Although they want to be appreciated, they rarely ask for payment. Although they want to win, they don't want others to feel bad about losing. It is a razor's edge they walk. For that reason, many Crusaders think of themselves as loners who are fighting battles for those they love independent of others' expectations. Table 12.3 gives a short summary of the Crusader style.

Table 12.3   The Crusader Punch Down

Complementary Versus Contrasting Balance	Preferences Versus Vulnerabilities	Impact on Resiliency
• Primary style = Romantic • Complementary Style = Warrior • Contrasting Styles = Mastermind and Expert	• Fiercely loyal to others. • Fights for causes that they believe in and benefit people. • May not recognize/surrender a losing "fight."	• Prefers respect and quiet appreciation. • Likes to be valued for their devotion to cause and people. • May burn out or become resentful do to their sacrifice.

EXTRACTING ME WORKSHEET

There is so much more to be gleaned from your assessment results. Once you have read through the sections of this chapter that reflect your results, write out your evaluation of your scores on the Extracting Me Worksheet. As a Romantic, I know you will commit a deeply thoughtful and emotional perspective to this exercise. Be sure to put your own needs first for once and don't be afraid to boast about those qualities of which you are proud. As a fellow Romantic, I have provided an example of evaluating your assessment in Chapter 15.

Chapter 13 Punching Down the Mastermind Style Influence on Me

Wine knows that having passion for life is an art itself.

– *Talismanist Giebra*

For a guy who has spent nearly his entire professional career in pursuit of a better understanding of how *people* think and interact, I am pretty sure that I'm fonder of animals. Nothing personal; people have a lot of very admirable qualities. It's just that they're so complicated. They often have hidden agendas, unspoken motives, and debilitating scars. Animals are much more transparent. I have always enjoyed the simplicity of their existence. If I wrote a book called *The Power of Understanding Dogs,* it would surprise me if even one dog would read it – for many reasons. But I do think that animals have interactive styles, too.

I also think that we humans could learn a lot from animal behavior. Just the other day, after spending several hours doing "ranch chores" around our property, I plopped down on our porch with a glass of Rosé. It was the first perfect day of spring, beautiful sunshine, high 60s, light breeze. I propped my feet up and sat back to bask in that feeling of a hard day of physical labor. As I slowly exhaled and sunk into the cushion of the chair, I looked out into the pastures to check on the horses. There they were: Mozart, Unico, Wally, Spicy T, and a cow . . . what? Wait a minute. What the hell?

Important note to insert here – we don't have a cow. We have four horses, two dogs, two cats, and an involuntary and unwanted badger sanctuary in one of our pastures that we have not mustered the courage to address. We have two extremely amorous frogs in our pond, an owl who insists on rising at 4:00 a.m. each morning to repeat his only question of the day (yep, "Who?"). We have what seems like an unusually large number of pheasants that really confound me, since they have wings but are extremely reluctant to fly. On the other hand, they love to run, which they do poorly and in front of our vehicles as we drive up the driveway. We are a sanctuary city for gophers, apparently, as my yard is continually converted to a series of dirt mounds the likes of which would have driven Carl Spackler directly from the caddy shack to rehab. But you know what we don't have? A *cow*!

Fortunately, I knew immediately from where the cow came. It was a neighbor's cow. Now, *neighbor* means something completely different in Walla Walla than Chicago. It's not like the cow just wandered over in search of a cup of sugar or some flour. Nope, the presence of a cow on our land, leading our horse herd – a detail too humiliating to the horses to share in this book – would indicate that we had a break in the fence that separates our land. Muttering like Yosemite Sam in pursuit of Bugs Bunny (Google it, if you are under 40 years old), I put down my glass of wine, reentered the house, and announced to my lovely bride that we were on the receiving end of a bovine breakout. I stomped down the hill to the pastures and began the process of identifying how Papillon – that was my name for the rogue Holstein – was able to escape incarceration.

Much to my surprise, and increasing exhaustion, I could not find any breaks in the fence. I walked up and down our land searching for the flaw that launched Papillon's flight for freedom. Nothing. Puzzled, I switched to plan B: separate Papillon from his newly adopted equine family and secure him in the pasture next to his former brethren. To execute this option, my lovely bride and I would first need to enclose our horses in one pasture and isolate Papillon so we could herd her individually toward her own temporary living arrangement.

It is important to understand that we are talking about navigating four of our five pastures – since, as you recall, one of our pastures was currently occupied by a hostile enemy, the badgers – each representing roughly three acres of land. So, for those keeping score or laying bets on the outcome of this plan, we have four horses, two humans, one creative cow, and 12 acres of land. I know that cats are the gold standard for herding challenges, but this scenario must place in the top five most difficult creature movement projects of all time.

Despite 32 years of marriage, my lovely bride and I have not refined our joint herding acumen to a particularly functional level. We tried hand signs, quadrant assignments, and various movement management philosophies ranging from gentle coaxing to less than subtle threats involving the phrase, "Beef, it's what's for dinner." Finally, Papillon was alone in one pasture and the four horses in another. Now we had to direct our bovine buddy through the gate to the desired pasture adjacent to her brood – two people and three acres to thread one cow through one gate. By comparison to the previous herding assignment, this should be a cakewalk. (Well, more like a cow patty.)

For the next hour, Papillon sliced up our defense like Tom Brady playing the New York Jets. She would run between us, juke left when we needed a hard right, and was completely unfettered in the face of a constant onslaught of clear verbal cues and hand gestures. On the positive side, Lori and I are now really psyched by an idea for a new fitness program for agricultural communities. The working titles are Bovine Boot Camp, Holstein Hell Hour, or "Cow-diovascular" Training.

We re-grouped at the open gate to brainstorm ways that two people could outsmart one cow after clearly failing to do so up to now. Meanwhile, Papillon gave us one final long stare, uttered a "MOOOO" that was likely bovine profanity, turned around, walked to the fence that separated our land from our neighbors, stepped on the top and leaped over. Just like that. Like, the cow was saying, "If you would just stop running me around your freaking land, I'd be happy to go home." Lori and I were equal parts astonished by Papillon's athleticism and embarrassed that we had run everyone ragged during an event that our visitor had been in command of the entire time.

It was then I realized that Papillon was a Mastermind.

As we learned previously, Masterminds can be fearless in the face of risk. They enjoy ideas, possibilities and the excitement of experiencing things that are new. But, just as with the other styles, those characteristics don't exist in a vacuum. They are influenced by a secondary preference.

A MASTERMIND WITH A SECONDARY EXPERT (LOWEST SCORE C COLUMN, NEXT-LOWEST SCORE A COLUMN)

As an avid football fan, I watch the Super Bowl every year – for no apparent reason since I am a fan of the Minnesota Vikings. (Aside: As a highly superstitious fan, part of the reason for me writing that last sentence is the faint hope that by doing so I have just assured that the Vikings will win the Super Bowl in 2019, a few months after the release of this book, and make me look stupid. I will gladly accept that trade-off. Anyway ...) Since I don't have a rooting interest in the game, I am more interested in the commercials. That is not unusual; many people enjoy watching Super Bowl commercials. After all, these companies spend around $5 million or so for 30 seconds of airtime. What makes my fascination with the commercials less typical than the average fan is that I am watching for a very specific type of commercial. I am looking for the one that you watch with complete confusion and after which ask yourself, "So, someone walked into the CEOs office, pitched that idea, and got that sale? Huh." For example, imagine this conversation:

"Sir, our ad agency team is here to share their ideas about our Super Bowl ad," reports the dutiful head of marketing.

"Excellent, send them in." The CEO can barely contain his excitement. He can only imagine what $5 million can achieve in terms of product education and promotion for a brand new car release. As one would expect, the agency has sent their best talent lead by the agency owner herself. She is a legend in the field of branding. As they settle around the huge television screen, the ad executive explains the commercial.

"We open on a longhorn steer standing in the middle of the road. It is blocking the car driven by Matthew McConaughey. Matthew recognizes the bull as Cyrus. He contemplates what Cyrus is trying to tell him while fidgeting with his fingers. He arrives at the conclusion that he should take the long way."

Silence.

The discomfort for the head of marketing is palpable. He looks down, refusing to make eye contact with the CEO, thinking that a once promising career has just ended. He mentally updates his resume. Finally, the tension is broken by a perplexed CEO's questions.

"Um, so uh, do we talk about the car at all?"

"Nope," shoots back the supremely confident ad executive.

"How does Mr. McConaughey know the bull's name is Cyrus?"

"Don't know."

"What's the thing with the fingers about?" By this time the CEO is grasping for any clues of a greater, more elaborate meaning to the commercial.

"Don't know."

"So, is this like a series that slowly unveils a bigger story?"

"Nope. Stands alone."

Silence. By now the marketing director is quietly rolling his chair away from the ad executive in a not so subtle effort to physically and philosophically distance himself from her. The CEO stares at the ad executive. After several uncomfortable minutes during which the marketing director loses approximately a decade of life expectancy, the CEO stands up.

"I love it!"

That commercial ran in 2014. I still remember it. *That* is the brilliance of the Eccentric: the combination of a primary Mastermind preference with a secondary Expert preference.

It is interesting to contemplate the combination of conceptual sensitivity with a desire for details and accuracy. I am inclined to think of this style like an inventor: someone who has great ideas but also has a need to see them take tangible form. During my seminars, I describe the Eccentric as "the person who cures cancer but can't seem to explain it to anyone." If we are all delusional – and we know that we are – the Eccentric may live in the most interesting delusion of all.

Eccentrics are artists in the way architects or home remodelers are artists. They create with pragmatism. They have an affinity for the technical and the risk tolerance of an entrepreneur. Interestingly, a good percentage of the Eccentrics whom I have met are musicians.

Their contrasting styles of Romantic and Warrior can make them less aware of their emotional environment. This, in turn, is why they can be frustrated that others don't immediately appreciate or even understand the value of their creations. Their relative lack of sensitivity to logic can add a certain obliviousness to purpose, too. By this, I mean that they often engage in creative endeavors that do not appear to solve an existing problem. For the Eccentric, creation and quality are the point, not the opinion of others or the achievement of a goal. In that regard, the Eccentric is like a fringe musician, the free form jazz musician or the experimental rocker.

I always think of Johnny Depp's many movie roles. Has anyone tried so hard to be unattractive on screen and can't pull it off? Depp could easily have had a very successful career just playing heartthrobs and romantic leads, but he chose to be Edward Scissorhands. That is the mind of the Eccentric.

They are the embodiment of "marching to the beat of a different drum."

The Eccentric's resiliency is based on a balance of excitement and routine. They are happiest when exploring, but within a consistent and reliable structure. Like a sculptor creating in a workshop full of tools, they explore their ideas within the framework of a predictable environment. The pressure of results can erode their balance and the need to interact with others in emotional terms can confound them. Eccentrics are often more comfortable with their craft than with other people. Finally, I wonder how the combination of a preference for concepts (Mastermind) and pragmatism (Expert) works together. The former embraces risk, whereas the latter mitigates it. Does this complicated relationship with taking chances create internal duress for the Eccentric? Table 13.1 gives a short summary of the Eccentric style.

Table 13.1 The Eccentric Punch Down

Complementary Versus Contrasting Balance	Preferences Versus Vulnerabilities	Impact on Resiliency
• Primary style = Mastermind • Complementary Style = Expert • Contrasting Styles = Romantic and Warrior	• Unique combination of creativity and execution. • Comfortable assuming risk but works hard to minimize it. • May struggle to explain the value and/ or purpose of their ideas.	• Prefers freedom of ideas and consistency of processes. • May have a complicated relationship with risk. • Environments that require consensus building or immediate results may cause stress.

A MASTERMIND WITH A SECONDARY ROMANTIC (LOWEST SCORE C COLUMN, NEXT-LOWEST SCORE B COLUMN)

I have always had a special admiration for this combination of preferences. This is a risk-taking dreamer who wants a better future for the emotional well-being of others. This is the Social Reformer. Given that I am the Crusader, a style that fights for causes, it makes complete sense that the Social Reformer would appeal to me. They *are* the cause. They construct the possibilities that will lead to a better life for the people.

Unlike the Love Interest, who reverses the primary and secondary preferences, the Social Reformer is committed to a specific version of the future. Their comfort with change is augmented by the charm of their emotional sensitivity, a combination that can make them very persuasive. They are effective at gaining a commitment from others to the desired future state that they have imagined. "I have a dream" could well be their mantra. Remember Susan Wally – my mentor at Marshall Field's – the six-foot-tall, flaming red haired, human freak flag? Yep, Social Reformer. She had a self-defined vision for a better future for the employees of Marshall Field's. She was the Queen of Human Resources.

Combining a conceptual sensitivity with an emotional one can leave the Social Reformer vulnerable to challenges like logic and pragmatism. Their contrasting styles, Expert and Warrior, are the cornerstone for processes and productivity, respectively. The specific details of the idea and the plan to execute it can be afterthoughts, if thought of at all. One could argue that because they are not encumbered by the need to a path to their desired future state nor burdened by those specifics, they are then free to let their imaginations run wild. However, they do benefit by these considerations or at least by gathering the input of others who manifest this perspective.

Social Reformers thrive in loosely defined environments that encourage ideas and risk taking. They are likeable and respond to others who share that quality. They may not appear to desire it, but feeling appreciated for their dedication to the welfare

Table 13.2   The Social Reformer Punch Down

Complementary Versus Contrasting Balance	Preferences Versus Vulnerabilities	Impact on Resiliency
• Primary style = Mastermind • Complementary Style = Romantic • Contrasting Styles = Expert and Warrior	• Can be passionate originators and advocates for ideas that enhance people. • Believe that change starts with a commitment to an idea. • May overlook tactical and strategic issues that impact their vision.	• Thrives when allowed to dream of futures that are better for people. • Responds best to environments within which freedom of thought is appreciated. • May experience duress when faced with the restriction of compliance and/or quotas.

of others helps to minimize their stress. The Social Reformer may experience duress when faced with time and/or accuracy demands. Their resiliency is based on knowing that the world can be a better place and that those around them share in that optimism. Table 13.2 gives a short summary of the Social Reformer style.

A MASTERMIND WITH A SECONDARY WARRIOR (LOWEST SCORE C COLUMN, NEXT-LOWEST SCORE D COLUMN)

Arguably, the two most influential preferences – concepts and logic – combine in this style to form the ultimate entrepreneurial mindset. The classic definition of the entrepreneur is that of a person with an idea and a plan: The Adventurer. They are the swashbucklers of life – Indiana Jones, Lara Croft, Han Solo, Peter Quill, Captain James T. Kirk, and Amelia Earhart all rolled into one. Every time someone scores as an Adventurer, I am reminded of a grade B movie from my youth: *The Adventures of Buckaroo Banzai Across the 8th Dimension!* Admittedly, not a great movie; but what I love about it is the vocational diversity of the namesake character. Mr. Banzai was a physicist, neurosurgeon, test pilot, and rock musician. This made him uniquely qualified to address the existential threat to humanity known as the Red Lectroids from Planet 10. (Like I said, not a great movie.)

The beauty of combining preferences for concepts and logic is that you are completely unaffected – perhaps even oblivious – to things like the opinion of others and risk. My first real contact with this type of thinking came in college. Like many students, I was completely clueless about what curriculum path I should be on, floating around the liberal arts buildings like a gnat in a wine glass. This academic ambiguity made my mind quite susceptible to experimentation, and this manifested itself in many lifestyle choices that shall not be revealed in this book. Suffice it to say, I was hanging with a diverse crowd. Some were a bit unsavory, but most were incredibly interesting.

During this period in my life, I dabbled with the idea of being either a rock star or a film director. (These options make a lot more sense if one alters their cognitive state sufficiently with a sundry of intoxicants.) Anyway, the former aspiration, that of rock stardom, was encouraged by a clear Adventurer named Donnie. He was a guitarist with an affinity for punk music – the perfect genre of rock and roll for four guys with varying degrees of little to no talent. Falling in the latter category, I was obviously the singer. The singer, in a punk band, requires no actual talent beyond the capacity to jump up and down for two straight hours while failing to enunciate one word.

We were the New Losers. We created an entire fake backstory of being the reunited version of the Losers with entirely new members. I remember us finding this whole idea to be hilarious. Others failed to see the humor. (It probably required that aforementioned delicate combination of intoxicants to understand.) Anyway, we would cover classic country and rock songs using a sort of punk reggae thing. We fancied ourselves a Midwestern version of the Clash. As with our humor, others failed to identify with our sound.

Donnie came up with the ideas, suggested songs, planned practices and –in an accomplishment that still boggles my mind – encouraged me to pursue time in a recording studio to document our . . . um . . . *talent*. Another friend – coincidentally, the other Adventurer in this story – was taking a class on audio recording and needed a band for a class project. Against my better judgment and surprisingly without the liberating effects of those intoxicants, I volunteered the New Losers for the gig.

And so it was that the New Losers arrived at the studio prepared with our two most rehearsed songs: "Jumping Jack Flash" done as a snarling punk anthem and "Cuban Refugee," a political statement done in reggae style. The latter had started as a cover of "Can't You See" (the Marshall Tucker Band song), degraded to "I Can't See" (our ode to those intoxicants), and it eventual became our hit single. Fortunately, we were so bad that no one could identify the rampant plagiarism in the performance. We were scared to death; in retrospect, I have no idea why. In our minds, we were way outside our depth. But Donnie kept us together. Donnie took charge. Donnie was fearless. Four hours later, the New Losers had a single with a B side.

That single, "Cuban Refugee," received consistent airplay on the college radio station. I would like to say it was because of the honesty of the political commentary combined with the sheer authentic and unvarnished enthusiasm of the musicianship. Nope. It was because I was the general manager of the college radio station. Still, the experience will always rate as one of the most exhilarating of my life, and I am certain I would have never done it without the moxie of the Adventurer Donnie.

Steve, the Adventurer who produced that recording session, was in my cinematography class. He and I were partners in a project to produce a film. It was the final exam of sorts, and the evaluation of this project would count toward one third of our grade. Despite what may sound like a rather loose commitment to academics on my part, I was very driven by grades. Remember my father? Fear is still a good motivator for a college kid. I eventually graduated magna cum laude, so being paired with Steve – whom I liked as a friend but feared as a project partner – was problematic.

But my fears were misplaced. Just as with Donnie, Steve had a vision and a plan.

I won't bore you with the filmmaking details of the *Double Creature Feature of Attack of the Killer Trash Cans and Milk Bottles from Space*. Suffice it to say that the creative special effects alone would have justified the A grade we received. More memorable for me was how exciting the whole process was. Just like the recording studio experience, I was frightened the entire time. Steve, on the other hand, never wavered from his idea and strategy. *That* is the brilliance of the Adventurer.

It is the Adventurer's contrasting style (Romantic and Expert) that allows vulnerabilities to emerge. Their relative insensitivity to the emotions around them can create issues with morale. They may appear ambivalent or even dismissive to what others feel. Their willingness to accept risk may make them susceptible to mistakes, and a tendency to look at the big picture and not the minutia can lead to inconsistencies. These are important considerations for the Adventurer when engaged in metacognition.

Adventurers are most comfortable in situations that reflect their name – exploring with a map. Being allowed the freedom to find their way and the independence to choose that path feeds their intrinsic needs. Conversely, their resiliency will suffer if they are required to build consensus for their ideas. Being managed too closely also erodes their mojo. Table 13.3 gives a short summary of the Adventurer style.

Table 13.3   The Adventurer Punch Down

Complementary Versus Contrasting Balance	Preferences Versus Vulnerabilities	Impact on Resiliency
• Primary style = Mastermind • Complementary Style = Warrior • Contrasting Styles = Romantic and Expert	• A talent for vision and planning. • Prefers a big picture focus. • Less interested in feedback from others and the minutiae of execution.	• The ultimate entrepreneur, comfortable with risk and focused on results. • Responds well to independence and freedom. • Stress can accompany situations that require consensus building and details.

EXTRACTING ME WORKSHEET

Whether you are the Eccentric, Social Reformer, or Adventurer, take some time now and reflect on your interactive style. Complete the portion of the Metacogntion and Reflection Collection Worksheet that relates to style. Remember, it is your interactive style that most influences your initial relationships with others. As a Mastermind, you may have a tendency to drift (heehee), so feel free to come back to this exercise often to fully flesh out your thoughts. And I know Masterminds may not want or need a model to comply with, but check out Chapter 15 for an example of punching down your style.

Chapter 14 Punching Down the Warrior Style Influence on Me

Either give me more wine or leave me alone.

– Rumi

The time/value ratio lurks like a specter in the consciousness of the Warrior. If your D column score is below 30, it is a constant influence on your behavior. If, like my score, your D column approaches 20 or even less, the force of its impact in large part defines you.

Warriors assess each moment of the day based on its value. You may not be entirely aware of this process, but I can assure you that it is taking place. It manifests itself in odd ways, ranging from the desire to continuously multitask, apply pressure to others to get to the point, the need to make "to-do lists to ensure productivity, and the ever-present search for metrics (scoreboard) to evaluate progress and results.

Despite my efforts to define my wander ponders as wonderful moments of Zen punctuated by the occasional burst of revelation, the truth is they are competitions. Sure, I use them to clear my mind, and by so doing, allow that vacuum to fill with new ideas and clarity of action. But my Warrior preference stands as an obstacle to true mindfulness. First, I list these events as "hikes" on my day timer (yes, I am old school). They are planned days in advance. Second, when I am home I take my wander ponders at the same place, Bennington Lake, each time. Although it is a beautiful area in Walla Walla, the reason for selecting the same location is so I can monitor my pace. I have identified three different hiking loops: a 5K, a four-mile, and a five-mile hike. Depending on my time constraints and general physical status, I can choose the best loop. For all three, I have identified mileposts. These mileposts reflect a specific point in each hike where I evaluate my speed by checking the time elapsed when I arrive at this spot. None of this sounds especially Zen.

Although the constant evaluation of the value of time invested may seem like a burden, it is exceptionally useful to the Warrior. It drives them to get things done. It is conducive to continuous improvement. It shapes their need to evaluate success and to think critically about processes. Now, it also is accompanied by some drawbacks: impatience, competitiveness, the inability to suffer fools gladly, and a tendency to be very direct when communicating with others. I also think my strong Warrior preference has required me to be more aware of listening skills, an important metacognitive revelation a few years back.

After our first child was born, my lovely bride accepted the position of director of domestic affairs. Stay-at-home mom (the common vernacular of the time) did not seem to capture the wide ranging and all-consuming responsibilities that a parent undertakes when she or he runs a household and raises children while their spouse continues to work outside the home. Each day I would come home from work and inquire about her day – and I was genuinely interested in this account. After all, these were the two loves of my life. And yet, within a few minutes of Lori recounting the daily activities, I found my-self mentally drifting to other thoughts – particularly related to tasks that I needed to get started. It was as if my own time/value ratio evaluator had assigned a specific number of minutes for Lori's update; an allocation that was far less than Lori's account of her day would take. Rightfully, she grew annoyed when she became aware of my drifting interest. My Warrior preference was irritating her Romantic/Mastermind style. And my Romantic preference felt bad that I was doing this.

Four things helped to alleviate this disconnect. I say "helped" because, as the saying goes today, "the struggle is real." Although I have not completely eliminated my tendency to get distracted by my need to "be productive" (as if listening to Lori's day isn't), I have become a much better listener by employing these strategies.

First, I make sure that my to-do list is always current. Some-how, knowing that the tasks that I believe need to be completed comprehensively listed on this document reassures my mind that I will accomplish what is necessary within the expected time frame.

Second, I remove all other distractions. Whereas Master-minds are distracted by their own ideas, Warrior can be dis-tracted by opportunities to multitask. They are confident in their ability to selectively listen while also working on the com-puter, watching television, checking their phone, paying bills, etc. The truth is that one can only listen effectively if one only focuses on that act. I learned to set aside all other tasks and focus entirely on listening.

Third, and perhaps this is unique to me, I encourage Lori to share her day as if it was a story that unfolded on chrono-logical order. This seems counterintuitive to the Warriors pre-ferred bullet point style of summaries. I wanted context, order, and elaboration. Perhaps it was my Romantic style that craved the emotional content. Warriors who are not influenced by a Romantic preference may not experience this same dichotomy.

Finally, and this is true of all Warriors, I had to learn to listen simply to understand, not to contribute. Contributing, generally in the form of "helpful advice" or topic redirection, was not useful unless it was specifically requested. My role was not to solve any problems or assign priorities to our dialogue. My role was to actively listen and understand what was being shared. Warriors are more comfortable solving problems with the necessary information rather than simply acquiring knowledge for the its own sake. I had to reframe my mental response from solution provider to sounding board.

So, if your assessment demonstrates a preference for the Warrior style, be proud of your ability to get results, think critically, and apply efficiency to most all of life's events. Also, be aware that your ability to listen to understand, not to evaluate, may be a critical developmental opportunity for you.

A WARRIOR WITH A SECONDARY EXPERT (LOWEST SCORE D COLUMN, NEXT-LOWEST SCORE A COLUMN)

This style combines a sensitivity for logic (efficiency) with a sensitivity for facts (accuracy). I refer to this combination as the Sage. The Sage recalls the seasoned veteran who has decades of experience in role that has many technical requirements. They can get things done on time and accurately because of both their knowledge of the details *and* their awareness of the shortcuts, cheats, and work-arounds that they can use to save time without incurring unnecessary risk. As we explored previously, the Specialist reverses these two preferences – which makes them most sensitive to accuracy and therefore more cautious as they refine processes. The Sage is more sensitive to results, which provides them more willingness to apply pressure to processes to yield more production. This subtle difference is important.

I was reminded of the Sage's style at a recent speaking engagement. I was the last speaker of the day. My client had invested in copies of my book for each attendee. Knowing that things would be a bit chaotic after the session ended and wanting to distribute the books to each participant, they decided to place the books on the tables at which the attendees sat. It made sense to me.

During the seminar, the attendees completed the assessment. One of the most anticipated moments in the seminar is the "reveal" of what the results mean. After 23 years and over 2,000 seminars, I still get excited about having the participants stand for each of the categories. This typically occurs after a break. Since the time it takes to complete the assessment varies slightly among everyone, I instruct them to complete the assessment, take a break, and reconvene in 20 minutes. Of course, it was the Sage who would use the 20 minutes to research their results in a copy of the book at their table. The combination of results and knowledge conspired to undermine my plan to build anticipation. It made me laugh. I was half surprised that the Sage didn't leave after they had sufficiently understood their own style.

The Sage's contrasting balance falls in the Romantic and Mastermind preferences. Sages are not known to be flexible nor diplomatic. When one is pursuing a speedy result using an efficient process for which they may know of few hacks to quicken the pace, the last thing they would seek is consensus or input. Balancing their "need for speed and process" with some space for discussion of morale issues and new ideas can be of great value to the Sage. Although the adage of the Sage may be "it's not personal, it's business," the effect of that on employee motivation can be detrimental.

From a resiliency standpoint, the Sage thrives when allowed independence to achieve results in a consistent and structured environment. Too much "meddling" from others or situations that become unpredictable or unreliable can create chronic stress. For the most part, the Sage appreciates strong processes; however, unyielding requirements of compliance to the detriment of results can also cause them duress. The point, for the Sage, is to be *done* – and an efficient process is critical to that. That process should be open to refinement when the details get in the way of the result. Table 14.1 gives a short summary of the Sage style.

Table 14.1   The Sage Punch Down

Complementary Versus Contrasting Balance	Preferences Versus Vulnerabilities	Impact on Resiliency
• Primary style = Warrior • Complementary Style = Expert • Contrasting Styles = Romantic and Mastermind	• A gift for getting things done accurately. • Focuses on efficiency and execution. • Often seen as inflexible and even superior.	• Prefers well-defined metrics for compliance and production. • Excels in environments with static, objective measures for success. • Makes experience duress in "touchy feely" environments or when dealing with chaotic situations.

A WARRIOR WITH A SECONDARY ROMANTIC (LOWEST SCORE D COLUMN, NEXT-LOWEST SCORE B COLUMN)

Corporate executives often ask me if it is prudent to assess the interactive style of job applicants. This is a common practice among human resources professionals and hiring authorities. Typically, my response is "no." I firmly believe that anyone can be successful in any job – provided the organization supports his or her approach and so long as he or she has the skills and/or aptitude necessary to perform that job. "Hire character, train skills, lead style" is my mantra as it relates to the employee selection process.

However, there has been one notable exception to this guiding principle in my career. I found that for service-related business, the Hired Gun (lowest score D column, next lowest B column) is a great style.

Like the Crusader, the Hired Gun uses both logic and emotion when communicating. This cocktail of pathos and logos is intoxicating and compelling. The Hired Gun is not easily dissuaded from their goals; yet they're simultaneously able to monitor the emotional reaction their pressure is eliciting. Although all Warriors are applying pressure to achieve a result, the Hired Gun is also monitoring the feelings of those around him or her to ensure that relationships are not damaged. Romantics tend to create long-term relationships with clients, whereas Warriors deliver rapid results. Combining those two capabilities makes for a very attractive approach. Further, the Hired Gun, being primarily Warrior, will deliver on the result they desire; the Crusader, being primarily Romantic, may be more prone to self-sacrifice.

This is not to say that if you are a Hired Gun, you should go into sales. Many a motivational speaker has proclaimed that all of us are already in sales . . . selling ourselves, our ideas, our perspectives. The Hired Gun's style is a persuasive one and influence is an important part of many vocations and life events.

Though the Hired Gun combined two very different styles (Warrior and Romantic) like the Crusader, the primary Warrior style helps to insulate them from the stress that accompanies that dynamic. With a clear goal and strategy, the Hired Gun uses their sensitivity to emotion as a monitoring tool rather than a basis for their actions.

The contrasting styles for the Hired Gun are Expert and Mastermind. Hired Guns may devalue the details and usually need to take the time to assess risk. The role of risk can be ambiguous in Hired Guns' choices. They are driven by the need to win while not damaging the relationships around them. Think of it as the creation of a sustainable approach to victory within which the people around them remain supportive of the Hired Gun's desired outcomes. Either side of the risk spectrum is not an immediate consideration. As a result, Hired Guns may not naturally be driven by the caution that leads to accuracy and quality processes like an Expert, nor the excitement of discovery, experimentation, and entrepreneurship associated with the Mastermind. Having both structure and vision present in their pursuit of sustainable success can be very beneficial to the Hired Gun. The irony is that Hired Guns are often quite successful even in the absence of structure and vision, which can serve to deemphasize their importance in their minds. The reality, though, is that a Hired Gun who augments their natural style with the appropriate systems and processes and is stretched by a vision for an even greater desired future state can achieve even more success.

It does not feel natural for the Hired Gun to pursue structure and vision. They are most resilient when working independently and being appreciated for their success. They enjoy the status that comes with being the best and may feel confined by the policies and procedures designed to make their contribution more consistent and reliable. And though they seek independence, they often do not possess the risk tolerance of a true entrepreneur. Preferring to pursue goals over vision, the Hired Gun can experience stress when directed by a conceptual pursuit rather than a strategic one. Giving the Hired Gun a tangible goal rather than a philosophical one is more effective in leading them. Table 14.2 gives a short summary of the Hired Gun style.

Table 14.2   The Hired Gun Punch Down

Complementary Versus Contrasting Balance	Preferences Versus Vulnerabilities	Impact on Resiliency
• Primary style = Warrior • Complementary Style = Romantic • Contrasting Styles = Expert and Mastermind	• Very persuasive without negatively affecting relationship. • Typically exudes charm and confidence. • May ignore rules or pursue results rather than vision.	• Thrives when appreciated for getting results. • Prefers goal-based situations. • May experience stress when not given clear direction or when being micromanaged.

A WARRIOR WITH A SECONDARY MASTERMIND (LOWEST SCORE D COLUMN, NEXT-LOWEST SCORE C COLUMN)

I first heard the term "specifier" when working with luxury appliance manufacturers. It had never dawned on me that the consumer draws upon their relationships with others when making large purchases. When determining kitchen appliances while building a new home, for example, the homeowners are likely to be influenced by family members, the builder, an interior designer, and the retail salesperson. Each of these people may have their own opinion, perspective, and agenda. I was hired by manufacturing companies to teach their dealer representatives to identify the style of these various specifiers, and help them develop strategies for presenting the value of their product line. In effect, I was teaching them how to influence the specifiers, who would influence the consumer.

With a sensitivity to strategy (Warrior) and vision (Mastermind), there is no more effective specifier than the Power Broker (lowest score D column, second-lowest C column). As I am fond of saying in regard to this style, "They possess clarity of plan and clarity of goal, and pity the poor person who says, 'I have an idea.' Idea time is over; doing time has arrived. Go do." As the name implies, the Power Broker has a relentless desire to achieve the desired goal as quickly as possible.

It should come as no surprise that many C-suite level executives manifest this style. At these highest positions within an organization, it is nearly impossible to maintain the depth of knowledge about the details that the Experts crave. From this viewpoint, the pressure is on achieving the outcomes that will best serve the organization, which can run contrary to the individual needs of those that comprise the company. The Romantic's emotional sensitivity can become a hindrance to decision making. All of this is not to say that neither the Expert nor the Romantic has no value at the top of the organizational chart; that is absolutely not true. However, it is also accurate to assert that a focus on strategy and vision – particularly within a capitalist system – is more *typical* at this level than a focus on details and morale. Rare is the company that pulls off the prioritization of all four.

So, as the Power Broker pushes relentlessly and strategically toward the desired future state, they may devalue the systems and processes designed to ensure consistency and reliability – a product of their contrasting style of Expert. They may, too, create some emotional duress by operating according to that "nothing personal, it's business" mentality – a product of their contrasting Romantic style. In my previous career as a Human Resources executive – and even now on the occasion that I am in the role of consultant – I have often found myself defending the decisions of Power Brokers. The impact on the day-to-day operation or the interim morale of the team are not their priorities; rather, they must focus on the likelihood of competitive advantages and, ultimately, success. The rest are the unfortunate casualties of war, so to speak.

To mitigate the Power Broker's blind spots, they are well served to have trusted advisors that remind them of the potential cost of their plans and goals. Individuals with a great depth of knowledge about the finer points of the process can provide some governance and protect them from unforced errors or excessive risk. Power Brokers can certainly understand the value of quality, even if it is not the first consideration when pushing for greater productivity. Power Brokers also benefit by having input relative to the emotional lay of the land. Understanding the impact of their ideas and directives on the morale of the organization can be helpful for crafting effective messaging.

Power Brokers work best in situations within which they have tremendous freedom and impact. As one of my favorite clients once told me, "I write the rules; I don't follow them." Efforts to unduly control or manage them will cause friction, as will overcommunicating or entwining them in activities that have little perceived impact or value. Routines can be stressful, particularly those that have not shown much in the way of useful results. In general, the best way to handle Power Brokers is to get out of their way. Table 14.3 gives a short summary of the Power Broker style.

Table 14.3   The Power Broker Punch Down

Complementary Versus Contrasting Balance	Preferences Versus Vulnerabilities	Impact on Resiliency
• Primary style = Warrior • Complementary Style = Mastermind • Contrasting Styles = Romantic and Expert	• A talent for getting things down creatively. • Understands the vision and installs strategies for getting desired result. • Often uninterested in the input of others or "unnecessary" rules.	• Prefers total autonomy to get things done. • Values flexibility and removal of obstacles to results. • Stress accompanies activities that are time consuming without commensurate value.

EXTRACTING ME WORKSHEET

Take some time to complete the "What's My Style?" section of your worksheet. Since you are a Warrior, this shouldn't take long (kidding). Take some meaningful time to consider how your style preferences contribute to who you are. Also consider how the styles that are *not* your primary or secondary preferences affect who you are. Remember, the most obvious component of who we are in others' minds is our style. For an example of an evaluation of style, see Chapter 15.

Chapter 15 An Example of Punching Down Your Own Style

My favorite wine is whatever is open.

– That guy

The more meaningful reflection you can muster for the evaluation of your own style, the better. That's why I think reading all the styles is a useful exercise. Your assessment is such a useful tool to guide your metacognition. Of particular importance is the order of your preference, but the type of pattern you display, the exact numbers, how close two numbers are to each other – all of these considerations can generate incredible insights.

Although skills, strengths, aspirations, and values are all important to who we are, none of those are as immediately noticeable to others as our style. Having a deep awareness and appreciation for our own style is critical to understanding ourselves and guiding our development. Later in this chaper, I will use my results to demonstrate what you can cull from the assessment. As I go over my scores, consider your own scores.

This may be a good time to review Chapter 5, "What's My Style?," again – and to keep in mind that there are no good or bad results. This assessment provides a tool for self-examination, not self-criticism. Right now, your goal should not be to determine what makes you great and what you need to work on. It is merely to identify you.

Be honest with yourself. We are undertaking an exercise in metacognition, and that includes understanding your own preferences, perspectives, vulnerabilities. Embrace you. There will be plenty of opportunities to create a path for self-improvement. For now, we want to understand our current state and recognizing our style preferences is critical to that goal.

The critical considerations are:

- What is my lowest score?

  This determines your primary sensitivity (A = facts, B = emotion, C = concepts, D = logic)

- What is my second-lowest score?

  This influences your primary sensitivity, providing it with nuance and broadening your perception?

- How close are my two lowest scores to each other?

  If you primary and secondary sensitivities are close, then both play a significant role on your style. If your primary is significantly lower than your secondary – seven points or more – then the influence of the secondary style is small. On rare occasions, a person can score a tie between their primary and secondary preferences. This dual preference phenomenon is a notable occurrence and one that is reflected in my own assessment below.

- Do I have a dynamic, nuanced, or common pattern?

  This was explained in Chapter 5, "What's My Style?" The distribution of all four numbers is an important consideration when examining your style.

- How close is my tertiary (third-lowest) style to my primary and secondary sensitivities?

This determines your ability to adjust even more broadly to people and situations without enduring large amounts of stress. If your secondary and tertiary preference both score under 30, your ability to expand to your tertiary style is strong. If your tertiary score is above 35, then you will likely endure high levels of stress when stretching into this perspective.

- How high is my highest score?
Your highest scoring column is your quaternary preference. Referring to it as a "preference" is a misnomer. Rare is the individual that can consistently and comfortably manifest behaviors and perspective that reflect their quaternary preference. The amount of personal duress that accompanies the use of the quaternary preference is typically sufficient to dissuade us from this perspective. The exceptions are individuals who possess a nuanced pattern.

What do you notice about your scores? Make some bullet points based on the questions above that will guide your self-exploration of style.

ANALYZING MY ASSESSMENT

To aid you in this exercise, let me use my assessment as an example. Here were my four totals:

A Column = 37 B Column = 20 C Column = 43 D Column = 20

- I have a tie between my primary and secondary preference: Romantic (column B) and Warrior (column D).
- There is a large distance in preference between my secondary preference (which in my case is actually two primary preferences) and my tertiary preference, Expert (column A).
- Although my pattern is within the common distribution, it is on the edge of being dynamic.
- Both my tertiary and quaternary (Mastermind, column C) preferences are high.
- My tertiary preference is Expert, quaternary is Mastermind.

By examining all these considerations, you can arrive at a much more thorough understanding of your own style orientation. In my previous book, *The Power of Understanding People*, we explored only the influence of the primary and secondary preferences without consideration of all these other elements. That's because this book focused on interacting with other people, and our relationships with others are most often transactional – occurring for a limited time in a specific context like leadership, team work, sales, and customer service. Even our relationships with family and friends pale in comparison to the level of self-awareness we can achieve. As they say, there is only one person who you will spend your whole life with. You. It is probably wise to know as much as possible about this relationship

After listing the bullet points that will guide your interpretation of the results, go back and write out how each of these areas influence your style. You will find helpful tools in the Extracting Me Worksheet. Again, using my scores, here is an example:

Reflecting on My Style

A tie between primary and secondary preferences is unusual. This, combined with the substantial preference for using these two styles rather than the other two styles, is a very important factor in understanding myself. Having dual preferences for emotion (Romantic) and logic (Warrior) provide me with a gift for both empathy and efficiency. I want people to be happy, and I will work hard to make that happen because of my need for both world peace and results. I am a directive counselor because I believe I know the solution to what is bothering you. I care deeply about my family and am called to action when they are troubled. Same is true about other relationships that I value. I would describe myself as fiercely loyal. Of course, that also means that when I feel betrayed or believe that my loyalty is not appreciated, this can create intensely negative feelings of resentment.

Not only do I have the unusual phenomenon of a tie, but the tie is between two styles that are exceptionally contrasting. This provides a complexity to me that can be hard for others to understand. My Romantic side values appreciation as an intrinsic need. I thrive when feeling appreciated and tend to "pay" others in kind. However, I also desire independence as an intrinsic need. Generally, Warriors prefer to be left alone to get things done efficiently and with a minimum amount of meddling from others. So, this indicates that I would prefer to be left alone to get results and reward others in the same way. This creates mixed signals to others as I vacillate between offering praise and space and require the same. It can also make managing my resiliency a challenge since my two intrinsic needs are very different. It would be hard to create an environment in which one experiences both ample appreciation and independence. Perhaps that is one of the appeals of my vocations as a speaker/educator. It offers me the praise of the audience and the freedom to move on to the next project.

I use tact and diplomacy to compensate for my impatience. As a result, people may be surprised by my intensity, as I tend to mask it with emotional sensitivity. Although I do not suffer fools gladly, I choose to hold my tongue and take on more responsibility to get things done. This can lead to overextending myself and then becoming resentful of my load. I prefer to be the rescuer rather than the rescued. Again, the influence of very contrasting styles as my primary preferences will make my interactive style more extreme. By this I mean that the differences between Romantic and Warrior are very noticeable and could create confusion in others depending on which style they have experienced with me: the Romantic tact and diplomacy approach or the Warrior direct and results oriented approach.

It is difficult for me to adjust to the Expert and Mastermind styles. Situations and people who are either highly structured and methodical or more systemic and unpredictable cause me stress. This contributed hugely toward my choice to leave the corporate world and pursue a vocation that limits my exposure to others. Over the long haul, I work best by myself or with individuals that share my style preferences. I don't think it is an accident that I have become fixated on helping others develop better and broader relationships and valuing style diversity.

I have spent the past 23 years educating people on style diversity and evangelizing the value of expanding your ability to communicate with different styles. Before that, I spent a dozen more years in leadership roles in corporate human resources development helping people appreciate diverse contributions. Since my own pattern suggests that I would experience that exact challenge, I am the classic example of "physician heal thyself." I don't think it's an accident that my passion in life is a direct reflection of my own vulnerabilities. I have worked very hard to be more effective in understanding and communicating to individuals who think differently than me. It is entirely possible that your passions, like my own, come not from your preferences but from your blind spots. I left the corporate world to pursue a career that would isolate me from people other than my events on stage. I live in increasingly rural locations. My scores suggest that a large percentage of my interactions with others will cause me duress. So, it's only natural that I would devote my professional work to The Power of Understanding People. It is akin to the doctor researching the cure to his own illness. Or, I'm a masochist. Or both.

Related to this, I will struggle with repetitive, structured activities. When considering the impact of interactive style on your essence, it is not limited to the people dynamics. Tasks and environments can be considered relative to their impact on interactive style. With my low preference for Expert and Mastermind styles, it will be hard for me to remain committed to mundane tasks, at least if I perceive them as such. This is especially true if I view them to have little value. I have signed 400 books at an event, a task that involves writing "Laugh and Learn! Dave" for nearly three hours. However, this task results in giving people the gift of my book. That's a very Romantic scenario. And it means I sold 400 books. The Warrior in me can endure this task, given the resulting sales! As with all things in my delusion, the time/value ratio must be correct for me to invest the effort, but the value of making others happy is huge and will offset any time investment.

Conceptual thinking is also difficult for me. I remember the pain of "brainstorming sessions." The first rule of brainstorming is that there are no bad ideas. For a low scoring Warrior, that simply is not true. Oh, I understand intellectually that every idea offers merit and may provide a link to another, better idea. Warriors, however, can't help but evaluate the merits of an idea. An idea with no chance of a result is fundamentally unappealing to a Warrior. Warriors hate "spitballing."

The evaluation of my own pattern clearly reflects that I am a Crusader/Hired Gun. When presented with a situation or person that appeals to me emotionally, I will fight for that cause with no regard for the personal reward. Absent that emotional connection, I will require compensation for the fight but will still use empathy, tact, and diplomacy to achieve the desired results. My intrinsic need is for appreciation and independence. I will experience high amounts of duress when faced with highly structured environments/people or those who work at a conceptual level. I do not like loosely defined situations *or* rigid compliance and operate best when given the freedom to achieve a result and the appreciation for having done so. My passion (in my case, to help others better communicate and appreciate diverse styles) is a direct result of my own struggle to be more comfortable with different style perspectives. Even my lifestyle choices reflect a style of person that enjoys the company of others provided that he has the freedom to choose when it happens. As my father would say, "I love people, on my terms." I guess the apple didn't stray far from the tree.

This would be a good time to return to the notes you took when you read about your primary and secondary style preferences previously and see if you can add even more depth to your self-evaluation. Remember, you will find a section with some guiding questions to help you in the Extracting Me Worksheet. Again, it is useful to return to your assessment several times, because the insights can be limitless. The results are not static either. People can change. In fact, just like with the grapes that make the wine, they must.

PART FOUR
THE VINTAGE

Chapter 16 Veraison

The Evolution of Me

True love is like wine, it gets stronger with age.

– Farid F. Ibrahim

"Can people change?"

This is the question I hear most frequently after I speak – one that is asked out of sadness as often as hope. It seems that people are split on people's ability to change. The fatalists appear resigned to the fact that the stars are cast, whereas the optimists hold hope that humans can achieve better behaviors. Even more interesting, when I ask people about what they *want* to change, I realize that they are referring to someone else. Rarely do people feel the need to change *themselves*. Of course, the irony in that is the only person that we can change is ourself. That is no easy task. As mentioned in Chapter 4, "Core Ideology," Piaget believed that much of our cognitive development was completed by the age of 22 or so. But, what if something important provided the impetus for a change after we achieved full cognitive development? Or, what if the mere passing of time and all that it entails could slowly guide us into new directions?

In the world of wine, the most wondrous moment of change is called veraison (ver-AY-zhun). During veraison, the grapes turn from green to purple. There are so many spectacular metaphors here for our own development. The grape is ripening. It is evolving to become a better vessel for making wine. Its contents become more appealing. Best of all, there is no clear explanation for what precipitates this evolution. It is a beautiful mystery. Without veraison, there would be no wine.

I believe the same is true about people – at least, the best of us. To reach our fullest potential, we must experience our own veraison. And, I think life provides us with the impetus to experience this transformation. Some of us recognize these moments and change; others of us do not. Or, more accurately, perhaps they do change but not in a way that maintains their desired alignment. Remember the graphic on organization alignment in the earlier chapter? As depicted in that chart, we are a product of life inputs, particularly those that we experience early on. Those life inputs don't stop happening as we mature, but their impact often does. Fortunately, we still experience events later in life that have the force to initiate veraison. They have the force to bust the concrete of our minds. Fortunate, provided that we maintain our practice of metacognition and integrate these new inputs into our core ideology to align with our outputs.

Some of these life experiences are obvious and common. Getting married, becoming a father (twice) and losing my parents were all life events that had a major influence on me and are common to many people. Any or all of these can create immediate, thoughtful changes in our alignment. Although it is not certain, there is a very good chance that life events such as these (large changes in inputs) will require a change in your core ideology in order to maintain alignment. For example, most of us will experience the death of a parent. We will grieve, reflect, eulogize, and then move on with the memories of our loss. There may be changes in alignment needed, but without the conscious effort to identify how this input has affected our outputs we won't know the best way to adjust our core ideology.

However, for a few people, this experience may force a deeper self-exploration and a change in the way they orient themselves to life. These are people who manifest exceptional metacognition. In these instances, the life event (input) will initiate a veraison. For me, all the aforementioned referenced life events had a major impact, but not all prompted a purposeful reevaluation of my core ideology. Just because one has an experience of this magnitude does not mean that a person will fundamentally change. Our version of veraison most often combines a substantial input (life experience) with metacognition and commitment to new ways of thinking (alignment) to arrive at a new or modified core ideology.

Any of these aforementioned significant life experiences have the capacity to stimulate veraison. On the other hand, many times our veraison occurs slowly and nearly imperceivably and is not the result of a purposeful alignment but rather a subconscious one. When I was younger, for instance, my tertiary interactive style preference was Mastermind, based on my MBTI results (INTJ) and my clear tolerance for risk, loosely defined situations, and new experiences. I didn't really have much to lose, so I had little sensitivity to taking chances. As I aged, got married, had children, accumulated assets, my willingness to accept risk diminished. Also, having spent the past 23 years traveling around the world nearly 200 days annually, the reassurance of routines became more appealing and the attractiveness of new experiences diminished. Slowly my Mastermind preference dropped and was replaced by my Expert as my tertiary style. Although this doesn't represent a quantum leap in change, it does provide me with an understanding of why I am less open to new ideas and more likely to fall into patterns now than I was in my youth. The style change was a long, subtle evolution of my core ideology brought about by a change in inputs and outputs over time.

Ultimately, what stimulates veraison in you may range from the glacier-like trends over decades to the flash points of love, death, joy, or tragedy. Or, it could be a vampire.

A SHIFT IN PERSPECTIVE

In 1995, my lovely bride was working part time as a travel agent in Orlando, Florida. One of the perks of that profession is the occasional offer to experience a tourism destination at a substantially discounted rate so that said destination can familiarize the travel agent on the benefits they offer. These trips are referred to as FAM trips (short for familiarization). One such trip was made available to Lori from the country of Romania. So desperate was Romania for tourism that they offered a one-week, countrywide tour at no cost to the travel agent. That alone would have caught our eye; but the real hook was Dracula. The tour of Romania included visiting the region of Transylvania. Lori and I are huge fans of horror movies, so a trip to Transylvania bordered on a journey to the Holy Land for us. We jumped at the offer.

Without engaging in a discussion of Romanian history – a conversation that I am woefully unqualified to lead – suffice it to say that this was not a high watermark for Romania. The country was just a few years removed from the communist rule of Nicolae Ceausescu who had been executed with his wife in 1989 after being convicted of genocide by starvation. Six years later, Romania was struggling with a new socio-political system and a weak economy. When we landed at the airport outside Bucharest, the plane gingerly navigated the bomb craters on the runway. Armed security guarded the luggage area. The customs experience was akin to being processed into the Gulag system. It was frightening.

Fortunately, our tour guide and host for the week collected us almost immediately after we exited customs. This was not your average tour guide. Nicolae Paduraru had been in the Ministry of Tourism under Ceaucescu, heading up the

Department of International Relationships *and*, to our amazement, was the founder of the Transylvania Society of Dracula. We had struck gold.

Nicolae will forever be on my shortlist of the most gracious people I have ever met. His kindness and his intellect combined to make him an incredible guide. We were stunned that a man of such importance to the country would not only be our guide, but personally pick us up at our hotel. Upon transporting us to our first hotel in Bucharest, he invited us to a welcome dinner that night with the rest of the tour participants. My wife and I went to our room to rest, but were undermined by the excitement we were experiencing. We changed and got ready to join the throngs of people with whom we would experience Romania.

It turns out that a throng in Romania is eight people. One of those was Nicolae. Another was the bus driver.

Imagine our surprise that we would spend a week in Romania on a tour with a former leader in the Ministry of Tourism and founder of the Dracula Society with only four other people excepting the driver. We were giddy. Being giddy, however, was not the prevalent response by the rest of the group. Within a couple of days, the group was down to five – Lori and me, one other intrepid travel agent, Nicolae, and the driver. The slow decline in tour members seemed straight out of a grade B horror movie, particularly when your tour guide heads up the Dracula Society and you are traveling to Transylvania.

We left Bucharest to visit Sibiu, Sighsoara (birth place of Vlad III, aka Dracula) and Cluj-Napoca considered the capital of Transylvania. In each city, we were simultaneously enchanted by the charm of the cities and the people – while also being keenly aware of the extreme economic hardships. We watched children joyfully playing games they had fashioned out of pieces of tree bark and a rock. We realized that our life experiences growing up are tremendously influenced by the affluence of our country and how so many others in the world have such a completely different set of life inputs. It feels silly to say, but we understood for the first time – in our mid-30s – the nature of privilege. Neither Lori nor I had come from wealth, but compared to what we were witnessing in Romania, we had lived like royalty. This trip had already changed us. Romania was the motivating force for our veraison. Then, it was on to the Carpathian Mountains.

HOLY &#!*

To say that the Carpathian Mountains or Transylvanian Alps are scary is like calling Stephen Hawking smart. Perhaps it was the situation, the weather, the time of day, or the stories of Vlad III, but I don't think I have ever experienced such creepy geography. If it were possible to convert the experience of physical shudders and goose bumps into a landscape, it would look like the Carpathian Mountains. It is little wonder that Bram Stoker was inspired to create Dracula based on secondhand knowledge of the area. Imagine how scary the book would have been had he actually visited Transylvania. The five of us navigated the road through the mountains on our modest tour bus on our way to our final hotel stay of the trip: The Hotel Castel Dracula (insert ominous music).

Arriving at this hotel after dark, in Transylvania, during a thunderstorm is almost otherworldly – or completely otherworldly. Now, to be clear, this is not Bran Castle. This is a rustic building – part castle, part old hotel – that had the good sense to brand itself as Dracula's Castle. I now know that the structure was built only 12 years before and in retrospect, we were basically experiencing a themed up version of a Hampton Inn. But given the situation, we were pretty sure we were entering the location of our untimely demise. And what followed did nothing to dispel that feeling.

Knowing Lori's and my fascination with the legend of Dracula, Nicolae invited us to join him for a tour of the crypt. *A tour of the crypt.* You know that moment when you are presented with a very bad idea and you turn to the love of your life and your eyes meet and you telepathically say, "That is such a bad idea, but I really want to do it"? Of course, we said yes. One hour later, we met Nicolae in the lobby and followed him to a remote area of the hotel. Nicolae unlocked a heavy wooden door, lit a torch and headed down a long, narrow, stone staircase. Lori followed. I brought up the rear in near darkness.

The light disappeared momentarily as Nicolae turned a corner and entered an empty chamber. Dirt floors and stone walls contained a space of 10 feet by 10 feet. It was empty with one notable exception: the coffin.

Let's pause here to review. Lori and I are alone in a crypt in the basement of a castle, lit only by a torch held by the founder of the Society of Dracula in Transylvania. That is a complete butt pucker moment. And yet, it hadn't even gotten *that* scary for me – yet. That happened next.

As Nicolae, by the tiny little light of that torch, stood at one side of the room discussing the legend of Dracula, I decided to do what my Y chromosome demanded. I decided to open the casket. Now, if you are a fan of horror movies, you know that there exists in all of them that *one character* who decides that the stupidest of all actions is the correct one to choose. I never realized that I was that character. Anyway, I made my way over to the coffin waiting to be admonished by Nicolae. He did not stop me. Eventually, I was standing right next to Dracula's eternal resting spot.

I hesitated. My heart raced.

I reached under the lid of the coffin and pulled up.

I have never been able to adequately re-create verbally what I experienced in this next moment. I always feel compelled to explain that I am a salt of the earth, Midwestern pragmatist who, while fascinated by the notion of the supernatural, is not ready to believe in what I have not personally experienced. Although I am emotionally sensitive, I am outwardly guarded, a remnant of my being raised by a stoic father. I am not prone to exaggeration, fantasy, or hallucination. What happened in that moment is as certain to me as the existence of the laptop on which I type these words.

The moment that I began to lift the casket's lid, a thin, pale appendage curled out from under the top and held it shut. I refer to it as an appendage rather than a finger because it bent more like a caterpillar than a finger. It seemed jointless. It stopped the lid's movement immediately. It had the opposite effect on me. I shot back like I had been shot out of a cannon. I have never, *never* experienced that degree of abject fear. Lori, who had been focused on Nicolae, caught my retreat out of the corner of her eye. I watched the coffin for further movement. None came.

Within a few moments, Nicolae finished his story and turned to walk us back up the stairwell. Lori quickly followed. The light was rapidly leaving the crypt, so I hustled behind them. We exited the crypt and left the area in silence.

When we got back to the lobby, Nicolae asked if we would like a cup of coffee. I thought surely the reveal would happen here. Surely, Nicolae would share the ruse that accompanies the trip to the crypt. Perhaps I had messed up the climax when the hotel staff member rises from the dead to scare the guests. Granted, I couldn't quite reconcile the malleability of the finger and it's completely unnatural appearance. Really good makeup on a double-jointed member of the bell staff? Maybe. A trained albino snake? Less likely. But surely, there must be some kind of final act to this hoax.

"Do you take cream and sugar?" asked a completely nonplussed Nicolae.

"Yes." I was looking forward to hearing how this normally works. I had just finished five years working a stone's throw from Disney's Magic Kingdom. I understand the notion of creating a fantasy experience. In fact, despite a much more unsophisticated technical approach, I was quite impressed with the level of discipline it took not to play out the big reveal.

"How is your room?" Nicolae continued this charade of normalcy.

"Um, are you not going to discuss what happened in the crypt?" Now I was becoming irritated. My blood pressure and heart rate had still not recovered from what happened less than 15 minutes before.

"What happened in crypt?"

"Seriously? There was somebody [something] in the coffin." By this time, I was incredulous.

"Really. How do you know?"

"Because I tried to open the lid and this finger like thing came out from under it and held it shut!"

You know that character in a horror movie who first sees the ghost (monster, vampire, werewolf, alien) and tells the police and they think he is completely goofy? I never thought I would be *that* character either, but here I was.

"You tried to open the casket and a finger from inside held it shut?"

"Yes."

"Well, people say they see strange things in the crypt." And with that, Nicolae sipped his coffee and changed the subject.

My mind was swimming. I couldn't reconcile what I had just experienced with what I knew to be true. Are they really *this* good at the scare? No American experience would leave the reveal unrevealed. Or did I just experience something paranormal? Is there something truly magical about Transylvania? For a multitude of reasons, I could not sleep that night. In many ways, my life would never be quite the same.

One of my crusades in life is helping people reconcile some distinctly human challenges: that we are all living our own delusion and that we believe our perspective is absolute truth (it is not) rather than a part of a greater truth. The Romanian trip galvanized this crusade. It made me realize just how much our life experiences shape our delusions and forge our perspective. It impelled my commitment to a career in promoting civil discourse, enhanced communication, healthy conflict resolution, and dialectical thinking. In many ways, the Leadership Difference, Inc. – my company – was the equivalent of my grapes turning from green to purple. It was Romania that pushed me beyond a desire to have a positive influence on the life of others and into a purposeful process of delivering on that desire.

IDENTIFYING YOUR VERAISON

Now it is your turn. Remember, your veraison involves three elements: input (major experiences in your life), outputs (what you value) and core ideology (how you align yourself to connect your experiences with what you value). The trip to Romania was a new input. It made me realize how limited our version of reality is and how important it is to broaden it. Civil discourse and understanding others' perspectives became a new core value for me (output). Perhaps it had always been, but this new life experience (input) had given me greater clarity and initiated veraison (change). It prompted me to put greater emphasis on finding ways to positively influence others by teaching courses on metacognition and dialectical thinking (more on this subject in the next chapter). It expanded my core ideology.

Time for metacognition and reflection. Ask yourself these questions:

- What major life experiences (inputs) have occurred to me since adulthood?
- How did I react to these experiences?
- How did these experiences change what I valued (outputs)?
- Did I change my core ideology as a result of these experiences? If so, how? If not, why?
- What changes in my core ideology would I make now, having reflected on these life events more?

Just as veraison's trigger is a mystery, so is ours. Sometimes a major life experience will *not* provide a substantial change in our core ideology. Don't be hard on yourself. I burned out of three careers before I had my chronic-stress veraison. As the saying goes: when the student is ready, the teacher appears. Quitting three jobs because I couldn't manage stress were significant life inputs. I remember engaging in metacognition – long before

I knew of the term – before, during, and after each of these events. Still, I did not commit to a meaningful change in my core ideology until that fateful meeting about the employee opinion surveys back in 1995. Not coincidentally, Romania happened later that year, further defining my veraison. Apparently, 1995 was a good vintage for Dave Mitchell.

Chapter 17 Age-Worthy

Maintaining the Best Me

Like fine wine, you get better with age.

*– At least one Facebook post on your
birthday after the age of 40*

We have come a long way. At this point, we've learned what metacognition entails, and then engaged in that process to deeply explore many aspects of our essence. We have taken responsibility for this journey and what we discovered along the way by manifesting an internal locus of control. We used the principles of horizontal alignment from organizational development to identify the important life inputs that have shaped our behaviors, both good and bad, and formed our current state. We examined our core values and desired outputs. We connected our current state to our desired future state with a core ideology that defines our vision and mission in life. If you have kept up with your Extracting Me Worksheet, you have documented all these episodes of positive self-examination.

That's not all. We evaluated our style. For many of you, this may have been a review of these concepts but with a fresh perspective turned inward. For others, this may have been the first time you have dissected your own preferences when experiencing the world. Either way, you spent meaningful time considering the influence of your approach to life on the definition of Me. We contemplated how these preferences contribute to our best qualities – and how they can make us vulnerable and oblivious, too. We even explored the complicated role stress plays in our lives. Most recently, we talked about our own veraison, our ability to change as the inputs and outputs in our life do. My hope is that it has been an incredible extraction process for you, filled with revelations, epiphanies, frustrations, and realizations – all culminating with a celebration of self. In that regard, this journey has mirrored life.

But we are not done.

BECOMING BETTER WITH AGE

The finest wines in the world are what we call *age-worthy*. Age worthy is literal in the wine world. It means that a wine is worth waiting for. Generally, that is cork dork talk for it will get even better with age. For us, age-worthy is a similar concept. Like the cliché in the quote that starts this chapter, it is important that we spend our lives in the continued pursuit of being better. The first 90% of this book involved me facilitating your voyage in self-discovery. Throughout it, I provided personal examples to help you understand the process. If you remember, *my* vision was to positively affect the life of each person with whom I come in contact. You may also remember that I am a directive counselor. So, did you really think I was going to let you get through this entire book without me allowing my Warrior side to have some time? Remember, my preference for Romantic and Warrior are high and the same. Translated, this makes my approach, "I want you to be happy – and here is the quickest path to achieve that." Just ask my kids.

Our final metacognitive trip involves some personal attributes that are crucial to age-worthiness. Just as a wine that gets better with age, there are certain characteristics that a person should display as time passes. These exist regardless of all the other variables we discussed. No matter your style, life inputs and outputs, core ideology, or locus of control, the best individuals eventually manifest these behaviors:

- A desire for lifelong learning
- The ability to engage in civil discourse and dialectical thinking
- A commitment to personal wellness

I wish I could tout myself as the embodiment of all three of these important elements of age worthiness. The fact is, like all of us, I am a work in progress. I will say that I can take a certain degree of pride in at least realizing the importance of all three and, despite protracted periods of my life that suggest the contrary, that they are priorities for me. Let's start with lifelong learning.

AN ENDLESS APPETITE FOR LEARNING

Academics have always come easy for me. I think that this initially had more to do with the fear of my parent's reaction to poor grades, combined with a developing Warrior preference, than it had to do with intelligence. Intelligence, in my opinion, is a lot more complicated than we educators would have you believe. It also may be less important. Academic success may be an indicator of high intelligence, but it's far from a definitive one. I have always aligned philosophically with models more like Howard Gardner's theory of multiple intelligences. Gardner theorizes that there are many forms of intelligence including musical, athletic, visual, verbal, and others. If you are not familiar with the work of Gardner it is definitely worth a trip to the library (or Google search). I particularly like that Gardner lists Intrapersonal Skills – which is essentially metacognition – as one of the forms of intelligence. In short,

I have always believed we place too much emphasis on academic performance as a measure of smarts. As a former high school athlete, I would marvel at the ability of a teammate to quickly learn a 200-page football playbook. That same person often struggled in the classroom. When the term *lifelong learning* is invoked by educators like me, many people associate the concept with their experience in school. For many, that is not a good association. It is unfortunate that the formal education process has turned off so many people to the importance of continued learning.

Remember Dennis, my best friend growing up? He was the co-creator of our homemade version of Strat-O-Matic baseball. Dennis was a fair to poor academic performer. His report cards were full of C's and D's. I didn't have to see the report card to know this, because I grew up in an academic system that flagrantly cast students by their "smarts." In grade school, our class of just under 100 kids was separated into four sections in each grade. If you were the best academic performers (receiving mostly A's on your report card), you were assigned to group 1. The above average academic performers – B students – were assigned to group 2. Group 3 was for the below average performers (C's and D's on the report card). If you were in group 4, you had the modern version of the scarlet letter D for "dumb" sewn to your clothes. This meant that our classmates spent the exceptionally fertile cognitive development period between the ages of 7 to 12 being assigned to the academic group that corresponded to educators' perception of one's "intelligence." Dennis was in group 3. I am convinced it was a life input that convinced Dennis that he was not smart.

Except, he is. *Very* smart. Although that system of labeling children at a young age may have imprinted Dennis' belief system, it could not – and did not – alter his *actual* cognitive talents. Dennis didn't go to college, I believe in large part because the system convinced him that advanced education made no sense for him. Instead, he was encouraged into vocational curriculum. After high school, when I went on to get my Bachelor of Arts in mass communication and business administration, Dennis remained in Greenup and worked for my father. Dennis quickly became invaluable to my Dad and his business. As my Dad's cognitive abilities started to deteriorate, the result of several undiagnosed transient ischemic attacks, it was Dennis who kept the business viable.

Dennis eventually moved away, worked in the Pacific Northwest in HVAC and effectively retired around the age of 50. Today, he works the summer at mountain resorts for six months and takes the rest of the year off. He has no debt, he has no boss – and only a nasty bout of cancer that he fought successfully has interrupted his dream life. His only regret was that he would have liked to be a meteorologist but lacked the education. And he only lacked the education because he believed the label given to him by a system with a narrow definition of intelligence. In all my travels, I have found no person more intelligent than Dennis – particularly if you define intelligence broadly.

Conversely, I know a lot of people who can cite some incredible evidence that they are intelligent using the narrow definition. I have worked with people with advanced degrees from Ivy League schools. I know people who boast of IQ scores above 140. Many of these people are exceptionally bright and accomplished. But others are not. Ultimately, it is not a degree from a school or a pedigree from a job that determines the quality of the intellect. It is the desire to learn. If you aspire to continually learn, you will always be intelligent. And, you will always be your best you. The most age-worthy people are those that continue to exhibit intellectual curiosity and a desire to learn throughout their entire lives. This desire also continues to create new life inputs that can influence your core ideology.

Twenty-five years after receiving my undergraduate degree, I decided to pursue my Master of Education Degree in global human resources development at the University of Illinois in Urbana–Champaign. It was a curious decision given that it was 2008 and I ran a business. 2008 was when the Great Recession began, and it did not seem like the best fiscal decision to invest many thousands of dollars on a degree when there was no indication this would result in a financial windfall. After all, most people return for advanced degrees based on the prospects of a better job and more money. I already had my perfect job, and this degree was unlikely to affect my income. But my decision wasn't driven by these reasons. I was becoming complacent, and in my mind, complacency equated to ignorance.

As a professional development goal, reading more books would be appropriate for me. I read – just not books. I read newspapers, magazines, online stories, blogs, and social media links. I rarely read books. I am embarrassed by that fact. A large reason for that is self-discipline. Though I know I *should* read books, I always prioritized something above reading books. If I were going to learn something, I needed some external mechanism to hold me accountable. Returning to a formal education setting made sense for me.

I won't pretend that I enjoyed everything about the process of getting my graduate degree. It had been a long time since I had to read so much information in which I had so little interest. But I learned so much. I felt so much more engaged. My perspective expanded. It took me just over two years to finish my degree, and I was so energized by the experience that I served as an adjunct professor and mentor to other students who enrolled in the program. I can honestly say that experience in my late 40s provided the motivational catalyst for my next decade of work. It both reaffirmed and reignited my passion for having a positive affect on others. Lifelong learning is that powerful.

You don't have to return to a formal education setting to be a lifelong learner. Maybe you are blessed with the desire to read. Heck, you are reading now. Some of the most impressive lifelong learners are those self-directed individuals who burn through dozens of books each year. Others dive head long into hobbies that further their knowledge. My wine education is an example of this form of lifelong learning. Whatever device works for you, do it. What interests you? What have you always wanted to learn about? Sometimes, when I am doing research for my seminars, I will end up losing hours of time going on rogue Internet searches on topic, events or people that catch my interest. Lifelong learning is just developing a more formal and strategic approach to acquiring knowledge. Just as the wine continues to expand its flavor profile over time, so must we expand our knowledge. In fact, when you purchase age-worthy wine, you open a bottle every few years to see how the flavors are evolving. Lifelong learning is a lot like that – committing to a process that will likely result in your own evolution over the years.

CIVIL CONVERSATIONS FOR UNDERSTANDING DIFFERENT PERSPECTIVES

The second component to ensuring that we are age-worthy requires some background. Dialectical thinking is not a simple concept to define. A Google search on the topic is likely to make your head spin. As a philosophy, it is credited to Zeno of Elea, has influenced the renowned trio of Socrates, Plato, and Aristotle and was reinterpreted by Immanuel Kant, Georg Wilhelm Friedrich Hegel, and Karl Marx. With all apologies to my college philosophy teacher, I have my own simple way of defining dialectical thinking. And, of course, I have a story. It involves universalistic formal thinking, relativistic thinking, dialectic thinking, civil discourse, four friends, and eight martinis at a remote steakhouse in the mountains of Colorado. You know, just another Tuesday night.

The Bistro Boys were a brotherhood of four friends of vastly different sociopolitical beliefs that would gather monthly at their namesake restaurant, The Bistro at Marshdale, a rustic but amazing steakhouse outside Evergreen, Colorado. The group was composed of Barry (the artist), Mark (the entrepreneur), Wayne (the retired business executive), and me (speaker boy). We would discuss current events and personal dramas while consuming two lovely and expertly made Ketel One martinis each. The meetings lasted two hours and always included some vigorous debate about issues related to the topics making headlines in the nation. Each of our perspectives populated different space along the conservative to liberal political continuum. The conversations were lively but not contentious, enthusiastic but not angry. Our goal, although not expressed, was to engage in dialectical thinking as opposed to the other forms of thinking. When it comes to debating a topic, there are some fundamental approaches.

Imagine there are three ways to discover a truth. One might believe that one absolute truth exists and can be uncovered. This person would be a universalistic formal thinker, believing that there is a formal universal answer for any important question. Once one has identified this truth, then it is just a matter of educating other people about the nature of that truth. There is no need for debate, only for the uninformed to become informed. Conflict resolution becomes a process of the person who is right explaining that to the person who is wrong.

Another person may believe that there is no single truth. This person may approach all situations with "It depends." This is the nature of relativistic thinking. Employing this perspective, different truths can exist because the context that surrounds the situation differs. How can one apply one truth to situations that are so different? "It's relative," they would say. Given that the situations are not identical, how can the appropriate solution be identical? In this case, conflict resolution is merely agreeing to disagree since we can never fully appreciate how the experience within which the situation occurred impacted the truth. To each his own, so to speak.

Dialectical thinking presents a third option, at least in the way I define it. I view dialectical thinking as an extension of my previous contention that we are all delusional. Our behaviors make perfect sense *to us* and arise directly from the beliefs we possess and cognitive schemas we use to sort through our experiences. In other words, our own inputs, outputs, and core ideology influence our understanding of the truth. When we find ourselves faced with others who believe and behave differently from us about a subject, we are simply presented with a person who possesses different cognitive schemas about this issue. I don't believe that one is operating from a position of absolute truth while the other is wrong (universalistic formal thinking). Nor do I believe that there is no one truth and that both people are free to continue their own perspective (relativistic thinking). I believe that each will benefit by learning the other person's perspective, and that the full truth will most likely contain elements of each perspective.

To illustrate these three ways of thinking, allow me to delicately dip my toe into spirituality. Why not, I have already alluded to politics. Maybe later I can address sex and complete the toxic trinity of subjects never to bring up at a party. Anyway, an individual who is employing a universalistic formal perspective may argue that their religious beliefs are the absolute truth for understanding spirituality. They subscribe to a specific set of beliefs that they believe define God. Someone with a relativistic perspective would believe that there are infinite ways to express spirituality depending on the orientation of the individual. Live and let live, many paths to god, that kind of thing. The dialectical thinker prefers to discuss the different opinions in hopes that this dialogue will get us closer to an understanding of the truth. I prefer this approach because it encourages discourse and open-mindedness in both parties. Employing the other two approaches seems to dismiss the need to discuss our differences since a universalistic formal thinker is unaffected by another perspective and the relativist is content to coexist without being persuaded by the other perspective. Dialectical thinking is based on discourse.

Now, that is not to say that each argument has the same *merit*. People can be largely or even completely wrong. What I am saying is that they arrived at this opinion through a process that made sense to them and to appreciate what that is, one must first listen to what they say. I also believe that when people engage in true dialectical thinking, the truth has a much better chance of emerging, and viewpoints held that exist far from that truth become harder to maintain. All of this is based on civil discourse.

It is this last point that made the monthly Bistro Boy meetings so powerful. Here we had four successful individuals, each over 40 years old with long-held opinions, a wide variety of life inputs, outputs, core ideologies, and interactive styles sharing distinctly different points of view for two hours – and no one got angry. I cannot speak for the other three, but I know that my understanding of issues and appreciation for diverse perspectives was expanded each time we met. We met for over 10 years, and still do when I am in Colorado for an event. Granted, the martinis were a draw to the gatherings, but it was the exercise in dialectical thinking that provided the true value.

There are two notable advantages of civil discourse on extracting Me. A commitment to continually engage in a process of broadening your beliefs will help ensure that your core ideology evolves positively and inclusively. Civil discourse and dialectical thinking also makes us better role models. To be age-worthy, we must serve as mentors in our society. There is an obvious deterioration of civil discourse in our nation, perhaps the world at large. We are creating more echo chambers via social media that serve to feed our own confirmation bias and motivated reasoning. The danger in this is that it creates false truths for the universalistic formal thinker, beliefs that they will argue with confidence rather than seek to broaden their point of view. The relativistic thinker will too quickly validate these false truths as a legitimate alternate position.

When I was younger, my goal when I found myself with an opinion that was different from someone else's was to win the argument. Perhaps this is the Warrior in me. After failing to win many of those arguments over the years, I began to realize that trying to inflict your universalistic formal thinking on someone else's was a fool's errand. Now, I realize there are three options using dialectical thinking:

1. Listen and ask questions to better appreciate the other person's perspective.
2. Share your perspective in hopes you can broaden the other person's perspective.
3. Agree to discuss this at another time if there exists a risk to civil discourse between the two of you.

The important application as it relates to extracting Me is to be interested in this other person's view and pursue a better understanding of his or her perspective. Dialectical thinking does not require that you change your viewpoint, but it does provide the opportunity to do so. That is important to our evolution and our continued pursuit of extracting Me. Like the making of an age-worthy wine, the winemaker's philosophy evolves. It is rarely the first vintage of a wine that becomes the classic.

AGING WELL PHYSICALLY

The last of the trio of age-worthy elements of Me seems obvious. Though we have spent our entire time engaged in an evaluation of our cognitive space, we are just as much physical creatures. I have always imagined myself as existing much like the alien prince Rosenberg in *Men in Black*. You may remember that he was the tiny guy inside the head of a human-sized robot disguised as a New York jeweler operating the body of his human-sized robot disguised as a jeweler with a series of levers. They discovered him in the morgue when his robot face opened to reveal him near death. He delivered the critical message to Will Smith about the location of the Arquilian galaxy. Remember? No? Guess it was just me. My point is, I think of individuals as two distinct systems: one for thinking and one for utility. Our cognitive function houses our essence, but without the physical vessel we do not exist – at least as we understand existence to be right now. Although it's important to place much emphasis on the former, the health of the latter is also critical to our development. Further, our physical well-being influences our life inputs, outputs, and core ideology.

This all seems entirely obvious except when you take inventory of the people around us. We are not behaving in a manner that supports how important our physical health is to our personal development. I know this sounds preachy." It is not meant to. I am not a health nut, nor am I qualified to provide guidance on nutrition and fitness. We have already established my fondness for martinis and wine, so I will not be throwing any stones at those who choose some bad habits. My point is that being cognizant of things like diet and exercise as early in life as possible will pay dividend in your pursuit of age worthiness. Finding your sweet spot for good nutrition and activity is as valuable to your development as effective metacognition. Health related problems can significantly alter your desired future state.

After "retiring" from organized sports, I spent nearly a decade without any formal exercise program. In my early 30s, my lifestyle had become quite sedentary. Fortunately, I struck up a friendship with a neighbor in Central Florida named Terry. Terry introduced me to weightlifting. Much to my surprise, I loved it! We also played pick-up basketball, which I enjoyed but placed a heavy load on my body as I moved into my 40s. When I moved to downtown Orlando, I lifted with Michael and afterward we would play tennis. Eventually the wear and tear tennis placed on my body also became unappealing. I started running and hated it, so that was no go. So were kickboxing and spin classes. I later moved to the mountains of Colorado and supplemented weight lifting with hiking. That was perfect. I tried yoga, but that was a no go, too. I am *way too* Type A for yoga. In fact, I seriously injured my neck trying to do head stands. It is uber embarrassing to injure yourself in yoga. I did not return. I had a brief mountain biking affinity that was replaced by bike-path biking and then eventually dismissed entirely. You see, the point is to find some activities that you enjoy and make them a part of your routine. It doesn't even have to be a conventional exercise activity. I enjoy clearing our property of debris and dead trees, and burning tumbleweeds. After several hours of that activity, I am far more exhausted than after a wander ponder. Extracting Me is also a process of finding the best way to use your physical attributes.

There are many things I could do better. I am squeamish about doctor's visits and must be near death to seek out their consultation. I should get physicals more often. Although I eat healthy for the most part, I love Friday pizza night and the siren's call of a ribeye steak is impossible for me to ignore. We all need to find our sweet spot for personal wellness. However, to not give any thought into the influence that our physical condition has on our cognitive state is to ignore the obvious. As the saying goes, "there's no time like the present." The truer statement is, "the only time is the present." To be age-worthy, make commitments to your personal wellness that will work within the framework of your essence and keep them. You may be surprised that refining your personal health commitment may influence things like core ideology. I know of many people who changed dramatically because of a new or renewed emphasis of physical fitness. Even if your cognitive Me doesn't change, the likelihood that it sticks around longer increases by including this age-worthy element to your life.

When you order a vintage wine – one that has been allowed to age in a cellar before drinking – at a restaurant, the server often asks if you would like it decanted. Decanting an age-worthy wine allows it to stretch out, expand, and reach its full potential. Personal wellness is very much like decanting your brain.

A PLAN FOR GREATER ACHIEVEMENT

Every good performance evaluation involves a developmental plan. As a human resource professional, I recommend to my clients that appraisals focus both on documenting past performance as well as outlining some commitments to even greater accomplishments in the future. The commitments to the elements of age-worthiness are just such a developmental plan. By outlining ways to continue your journey with lifelong learning, civil discourse, and personal wellness, you help ensure that the best you will only get better over time. Just like that fine wine.

So head back to the Extracting Me Worksheet one last time and contemplate the trinity of age-worthiness: lifelong learning, civil discourse, and personal wellness. Construct a plan for integrating all three into your life. If they are already prominent in your world, good for you. You are well on your way to achieving the best you.

Epilogue Uncorking Me

We serve no wine before its time.

– *Orson Welles, describing Paul Masson wines*

I wrote my previous book, *The Power of Understanding People*, to assist the reader with the many professional and personal relationships that we all have in our life. "The world would be a wonderful place if it weren't for people," was a quote from my dad that started the book. So much of our stress originates in our struggle to understand the behavior of others. As I traveled the world speaking on those concepts, an interesting development occurred. When I finished a seminar on *The Power of Understanding People,* many of the attendees wanted to know more about themselves. I realized that much of the reason we struggle with others is that we haven't truly taken the time to understand ourselves. I also recognized how people are so eager to be validated by others. I knew that my next book would need to focus on helping others better get to know their Me. Living in wine country, the correlation between a vintner understanding the grape to make the best wine was the exact metaphor for our pursuit to extracting Me.

Each year brings different conditions of heat, sun, rain, and context to the vineyard. Although the roots run deep into the soil and remain constant, the grapes are influenced by the swirl of unpredictability in each vintage. The winemaker must begin with what *terroir,* the vine, and the weather has provided, but she can then begin crafting her masterpiece from her own clear understanding of her ideology, knowledge, and abilities. The trek from vine to bottle is a journey that starts anew continuously. Each year represents advantages and challenges. The inputs change, the ideology adjusts, the outputs may evolve over time.

We, too, are in continual flux. Like the fine wine that we open at our table, we are a product of solid roots, careful consideration, and craftsmanship, an ideology aligned, a style assessed, and an aptitude for aging. Interestingly, consummate winemakers keep meticulous notes about the vintage, the harvest, the crush, the punch downs, and the storage vessel. These notes provide them with a way to measure their efforts and continually improve their products. The most valuable tool for assessing the winemakers' labor is to taste the wine. In vino veritas – in wine, truth.

And so it is with us. Return often to these reflections and metacognitive exercises. Continue to take stock in your life. You will evolve and grow. Your life will change, for better or worse – because life doesn't give a damn, and those developments will need to be ruminated upon. The power of understanding yourself is not a moment in time, but an elaborate process spanning your entire life. You will need to savor the taste of it at each interval. To be our best, we must continually know what that is right now. In the words of Dale Mitchell, my cantankerous father, "We should be born old and grow younger because by the time we figure out how everything works, none of it does." Tick tock.

Cheers!

Extracting Me Worksheet

LOCUS OF CONTROL: BEING ACCOUNTABLE FOR ME

Consider an example in your life that reflects your use of an external locus of control that contributed to stress. List it and ask yourself the following:

- Why have I chosen not to manifest an internal locus of control on this issue?
- If I were to commit to one action that might positively affect this situation, what would it be?
- Am I ready to do that? If not now, why?
- Upon taking an internal locus of control action, how did this situation change?
- Did this outcome reduce my stress? Improve the situation? Why or why not?

THE CRUSH: THE CORE IDEOLOGY OF ME

Identifying Inputs

- In what ways did my parents contribute to who I am today? Siblings? Friends?
- What memorable childhood events or experiences have had a lasting impact on me?
- What successes in my past have made me the proudest? Why?
- What failures have I experienced that left a lasting impression? Why?
- What individuals have served as mentors to me and why?
- What characteristics in others are most inspiring to me? Why?
- What characteristics in others irritate me the most? Why?
- What are my happiest memories?
- What are my saddest memories?
- If I could change one thing about my childhood, what would it be? Why?

Identifying Outputs

List your top five core values and define each.

1. _____

  _____

2. _____

  _____

3. _____

  _____

4. _____

_____

5. _____

_____

Defining Your Core Ideology

Using the definitions from your five preceding core values, write your core ideology below.

_____

_____

_____

_____

WHAT'S MY STYLE? SHADES OF ME

My assessment results are:

Expert	Romantic	Mastermind	Warrior

- My primary style preference (lowest score) is

  _____

  o How would I describe the influence of my primary style on me?

  _____

  _____

  _____

_____

_____

_____

- My secondary style preference (second-lowest score) is

  _____

  o How would I describe the influence of my secondary style on me?

  _____

  _____

  _____

  _____

  _____

- Which of the three distribution patterns does this represent? (Dynamic, Nuanced, or Common)
  o How does my distribution pattern influence me?

  _____

  _____

  _____

  _____

  _____

  _____

- My tertiary style preference (third lowest score) is

  _____

  o How close is my tertiary style preference to my secondary style preference?

  _____

  _____

  _____

  _____

  o What does the relationship between my tertiary style preference and my secondary style preference tell me about my style?

  _____

  _____

  _____

  _____

  _____

  _____

- My least preferred style (highest score) is _____
  o How does that influence my overall style?

  _____

  _____

  _____

  _____

_____

_____

- What have I learned about my style as it relates to the following categories:
  - Complementary Versus Contrasting Balance

  _____

  _____

  _____

  _____

  _____

  - Preferences Versus Vulnerabilities

  _____

  _____

  _____

  _____

  _____

  - Impact on Resiliency

  _____

  _____

  _____

_____

_____

_____

- Write a paragraph or more about Me that summarizes all the information that you assembled about your style.

_____

_____

_____

_____

_____

VERAISON: THE EVOLUTION OF ME

- What major life experiences (inputs) have occurred to me since adulthood?

_____

_____

_____

_____

- How did I react to these experiences?

_____

_____

_____

_____

_____

- How did these experiences change what I valued (outputs)?

_____

_____

_____

_____

- Did I change my core ideology as a result of these experiences? If so, how? If not, why?

_____

_____

_____

_____

- What changes in my core ideology would I make now, having reflected on these life events more?

_____

_____

_____

_____

_____

AGE-WORTHY: MAINTAINING THE BEST ME

What is your plan for a new or continued commitment to each
of the following?

- Lifelong learning

_____

_____

_____

_____

_____

- Civil discourse

_____

_____

_____

_____

_____

Personal wellness

_____

_____

_____

_____

About the Author

Dave Mitchell is an internationally recognized, award-winning speaker on leadership, relationships, selling skills, and customer experience. He founded the Leadership Difference, Inc. in 1995. His popularity is based on his unique ability to bring humor and authenticity to proven business strategies and complicated applied cognitive psychology concepts. He is also a certified advanced wine sommelier, which is a far more popular topic for discussion at parties. In addition to this book, Dave authored *Live and Learn or Die Stupid* and *The Power of Understanding People.*

When not traveling around the world delivering "enter-train-ment" to his many clients, Dave enjoys tending to 20 acres of land outside Walla Walla, Washington, in the heart of the Washington wine country with his lovely bride, Lori. They have two adult children, Brooke and Slade, and a collection of animals of the equine, canine, and feline variety.

Index

Printed in the USA
CPSIA information can be obtained
at www.ICGtesting.com
JSHW012243160823
46674JS00001B/104

9 781119 516330